Magritte

Liberté • Égalité • Fraternité
RÉPUBLIQUE FRANÇAISE

Ministère
Culture
Communication

An exhibition organized in partnership with Air France and Dauphin

Magritte

Edited by Daniel Abadie

galerie nationale du **Jeu de Paume**

LUDION

Magritte

Paris, Galerie nationale du Jeu de Paume
February 11–June 9, 2003

Exhibition

Curator
Daniel Abadie

Coordinators
Véronique Dabin, with Katia Uytterhaegen

Registrars
Maddy Cougouluegnes and Jean-Luc Delest

Installation
Walter Pellevoisin, with Olivier Filippi and
Christophe Prat

Cultural programming
Michel Baudson

International relations
Frédérique Bruelle

Communications and sponsorships
Anastasia Denoux and Laurence Lissac

Press liaison
Eva Bechmann and Maya Salem-Merino

Catalogue

Translation
Donald Pistolesi and Caroline Beamish (Abadie essay)

Editing and typesetting
Paul van Calster and Anagram, Ghent

Design
Bernard Lagacé

Copyright © 2003 Editions du Jeu de Paume,
Paris / Ludion, Ghent–Amsterdam, 2003
Copyright © 2003 the authors
Copyright © 2003 Charly Herscovici / ADAGP,
for works by Magritte
Copyright © 2003 ADAGP, Paris / the artists, for all
other works of art

ISBN 90-5544-434-0
D/2003/6328/08

Printed in Belgium

This exhibition is under the patronage of

**Monsieur Jacques Chirac,
Président de la République française**

and Sa Majesté le Roi des Belges

Honorary Committee

Madame Georges Pompidou

Mrs. Eliane De Wilde
Mrs. Ulla Dreyfus-Best
Mrs. Christophe de Menil
Mrs. Sarah Whitfield

Dedicated to the memory of David Sylvester

Lenders

Paris has not seen a major exhibition of Magritte since the retrospective held at the Centre Georges Pompidou twenty-three years ago. In the intervening nearly quarter-century, Magritte's work has continued to gain in importance and resonance. If the exhibitions mounted at the Centre Georges Pompidou and in Brussels in 1998 for the hundredth anniversary of the artist's birth provided an overall assessment of the stature of this outstanding figure of Surrealism, the exhibition we are presenting aims to bring Magritte's innovative dimension to the fore and show how it has echoed through the avant-garde movements of the past forty years. Because an exhibition concept of this kind requires a very specific selection of works, we depended all the more on the goodwill of the lenders, who have been kind enough to part with works that are so frequently requested for exhibitions devoted either to Magritte himself or to Surrealism.

For this reason, we wish to express our very special gratitude to the institutions and private collectors who responded favorably to our request:

- Micky and Pierre Alechinsky
- Timothy Baum, New York
- Ivor Braka LTD, London
- Centre Georges Pompidou, Paris. Musée National d'Art Moderne / Centre de Création industrielle
- Collection Diane S.A.
- Collection de l'Etat belge, Ministère de la Communauté française de Belgique, Service général du Patrimoine culturel et des Arts plastiques
- Dexia Bank
- Mr. and Mrs. Ahmet Ertegün
- Frederick R. Weisman Art Foundation, Los Angeles, California
- Galerie Christine et Isy Brachot, Brussels
- Galerie Xavier Hufkens, Brussels
- Hiroshima Prefectural Art Museum
- Hirshhorn Museum and Sculpture Garden, Smithsonian Institution, Washington DC
- Hogarth Galleries, Sydney
- Jasper Johns Collection
- Konrad Klapheck, Düsseldorf
- Koninklijk Museum voor Schone Kunsten, Antwerp
- Kunsthaus Zurich
- Los Angeles County Museum of Art, Los Angeles
- Anne-Marie Martin
- Moderna Museet, Stockholm

- Jean-Yves Mock
- Musées Royaux des Beaux-Arts de Belgique, Brussels
- Museum Boijmans Van Beuningen, Rotterdam
- Museum voor Schone Kunsten, Ghent
- Collection Nathalie and Anouck
- National Gallery of Art, Washington, DC
- Peggy Guggenheim Collection, Venice (Solomon R. Guggenheim Foundation, New York)
- Leslee and David Rogath Collection
- Rose Art Museum, Brandeis University, Waltham, Massachusetts
- Gunter Sachs Collection
- Scottish National Gallery of Modern Art, Edinburgh
- Sprengel Museum, Hanover
- Staatsgalerie moderner Kunst, Munich
- Tate London
- The Berardo Collection – Sintra Museum of Modern Art
- The Israel Museum, Jerusalem
- The Menil Collection, Houston
- The Museum of Modern Art, New York
- The Robert Rauschenberg Foundation
- Virginia Museum of Fine Arts, Richmond
- Zwirner & Wirth, New York & Galerie Brusberg, Berlin

and those lenders who wish to remain anonymous.

Acknowledgments

To locate some of the works and secure their loan, we had to rely on the friendly offices of those who were close to Magritte and his work. In preparing the catalogue, which includes some previously unpublished documents, the assistance of a number of people was also invaluable. It is a particular pleasure to thank the following persons for their various contributions:

- Mrs. Claude Acaei
- Bill Acquavella
- Anne Anthony, Galerie Montenay-Giroux, Paris
- Robert Altmann
- Arakawa and Madeline Gins
- Juliette Armand, Réunions des Musées Nationaux, Paris
- Abigail Asher, Guggenheim, Asher Associates, Inc.
- Alan Koppel Gallery, Chicago
- Reinhold Baumstark, Bayerische Kunstsammlungen, Munich
- Alison Belknap, Katonah
- Sandra Benito Velez, Museo National de San Carlos, Mexico
- Ted Bonin, Alexander and Bonin, New York
- Adam J. Boxer, Ubu Gallery, New York
- Isy Brachot
- Monique Bréhier, Christie's Brussels
- Charles Byron, New York
- Sandra Calvados, Direction des Musées de France
- Richard Calvocoressi, Scottish National Gallery of Modern Art, Edinburgh
- Stéphane Campo, Campo & Campo, Antwerp
- Andrea Caratsch, de Pury & Luxembourg, Zurich
- Pierre-Etienne Champenois, Belgian Ambassador in Paris
- Christo and Jeanne-Claude
- Sylvia de Cuevas
- Patrice Dartevelle, Ministère de la Communauté française de Belgique
- James T. Demetrion
- Chris Dercon, Museum Boijmans Van Beuningen, Rotterdam
- Gustavus Dierckx, Belgian Ambassador in Japan
- Bernd Dütting, Galerie Beyeler, Basel
- Jean Edmonson, Acquavella Galleries, New York
- Nicolas H. Ekstrom, Ekstrom & Ekstrom, New York
- Aube Elléouët-Breton
- Olivier Fayt, Knokke-Heist
- Evelyne Ferlay, Galerie Jan Krugier, Ditesheim & Cie, Geneva
- Philippine Fischer, Kunsthalle der Hypo-Kulturstiftung, Munich
- Pauline Flach, The Mayor Gallery, London
- Marcel Fleiss, Galerie 1900–2000, Paris
- Kathleen Flynn, Acquavella Galleries, New York
- Bruno Fornari, Museum voor Schone Kunsten, Ghent
- Marcia Gail Levine, New York
- Hartvig Garnirus, Theo Wormland Foundation, Munich
- Arnold Glimcher, Pace Wildenstein Gallery, New York
- Elizabeth Gorayeb, Sotheby's New York
- Maurice Gourdault-Montagne, French Ambassador in Japan
- Susanna Greimel, Rupertinum, Museum moderner Kunst, Salzburg
- Pamela Griffin, Hayward Gallery Library, London
- Martin Guesnet, Briest, Paris
- Simone Guttman
- Renilde Hammacher, Brussels
- Patrice Henry, Editions du Centre Pompidou
- Scott Hodes
- Waring Hopkins, Galerie Hopkins-Custot, Paris
- Isy Horowitz
- Nicole d'Huart, Musée d'Ixelles, Brussels
- Xavier Hufkens, Galerie Xavier Hufkens, Brussels
- Brooks Jackson
- James Goodman Gallery, New York
- Jacques-Pierre Gougeon, Embassy of France, Berlin
- Guido M. C. Jansen, Museum Boijmans Van Beuningen, Rotterdam
- Patricia Jaspers, Dexia Bank, Brussels
- Maurice Keitelman, Galerie Keitelman, Brussels
- Samy Kinge, Paris
- Hansruedi Klinger, R. and H. Batliner Art Foundation, Vaduz
- Hélène Koutsodis-Iolas
- Jan Krugier, Geneva
- Sharon-Michi Kusunoki, Edward James Foundation
- Charles-Etienne Lagasse, Commissariat général aux Relations internationales de la Communauté française de Belgique
- Stefie Langui
- Denise Lévy, Paris
- Tomás Llorens, Museo Thyssen-Bornemisza, Madrid

- Glenn Lowry, The Museum of Modern Art, New York
- Nicholas F. Maclean, Christie's New York
- Hector Magotte, Echevin de la ville de Liège
- Daniel Malingue, Galerie Daniel Malingue, Paris
- Claude Martin, French Ambassador in Germany
- Massimo Martino, Mendrisio
- Takeshi Matsumoto, Matsumoto Co Ltd, Tokyo
- Beatrix Medinger, Viart Corporation, New York
- Meridian Fine Art, New York
- Isabelle Merly, Centre Georges Pompidou, Paris
- Zaïra Mis, Brussels
- Jean-Gabriel Mitterrand, JGM Galerie, Paris
- Jean-Yves Mock
- André Mourgues
- François Narmon, Dexia Bank
- Ruth Neitemeier, Galerie Brusberg, Berlin
- Roger Nellens, Knokke-le-Zoute
- Sarah Nelson, Christie's New York
- Claudia Neugebauer, Galerie Beyeler, Basel
- David Nolan, Nolan / Eckman Gallery, New York
- Gisèle Ollinger
- Marty Pazner, President of the Friends of Tel Aviv
- Sylvain Perlstein, Antwerp
- Monica Proni, Bologna
- Pierre Richard, Dexia Bank
- Ned Rifkin, Hirshhorn Museum and Sculpture Garden, Smithsonian Institution, Washington, DC
- Cora Rosevear, The Museum of Modern Art, New York
- Jacques Rummelhardt, French Ambassador in Belgium
- Phillip Rylands, Peggy Guggenheim Collection, Venice

- Liliane Sabatini, Musée de l'Art wallon, Liège
- John Silberman, New York
- Christine Sirtaine-Janlet
- Gianna Sistu, Galerie Gianna Sistu, Paris
- Professor Heinz Spielmann, Bucerius Kunst Forum, Hamburg
- Björn Springfeldt
- Ann Stewart, Videomuseum, Centre Georges Pompidou, Paris
- Kensuke Sugimoto, The Chunichi Shimbun
- Philippe Suinen, Ministère de la Communauté française de Belgique
- Danièle de Temmerman
- Alicia B. Thomas, National Gallery of Art, Washington, DC
- Togo Fine Art, Japan
- Patrice Trigano, Galerie Patrice Trigano, Paris
- Ronny Van de Velde, Antwerp
- Dirk Van Eeckhout, Consul General of Belgium, Osaka
- Sophie Van Vliet, Musées Royaux des Beaux-Arts de Belgique, Brussels
- Daniel Varenne, Galerie Daniel Varenne, Geneva
- Paolo Vedovi, Galerie Odermatt-Vedovi, Paris
- Dr. Christoph Vögele, Kunstmuseum Solothurn
- Leslie Waddington, Waddington Galleries, London
- Jeffrey Weiss, National Gallery of Art, Washington, DC
- Nancy Whyte, Nancy Whyte Fine Arts Inc., New York
- Tracy Williams, Zwirner & Wirth, New York
- Renos Xippas, Paris
- Christine Zehner, Gallery Edward Tyler Nahem, New York
- Bernadette Zervudacki, Embassy of France, Brussels

Among those who helped make this exhibition and its catalogue a reality, very special assistance was provided by:

- Geraldine Aramanda, archivist, The Menil Collection, Houston
- Eva Avloniti, Archivist, Impressionist and Modern Art Department, Sotheby's London
- Olivier Camu, Christie's London
- Geert Criel, Palais Royaln, Brussels
- Susan Davidson, New York

- Matthew Drutt, The Menil Collection, Houston
- Daniel Filipacchi
- Tom Krens, Solomon R. Guggenheim Foundation, New York
- Nicholas Serota, The Tate Gallery, London
- James S. Snyder, The Israel Museum, Jerusalem

to whom we express our gratitude.

This exhibition would not have been possible without the active and kind support of Charly Herscovici, President of the Fondation Magritte, who wished to see Paris host the work of René Magritte again and to have the Jeu de Paume organize the event. His involvement in the project and his support in approaching institutions and collectors were a constant aid. We extend to him our warmest thanks.

Contents

Michel Butor

The Catalogue of Encounters
Complainte de Magritte

for Daniel Abadie

I want to surprise you
by using
the simplest of words
schoolday memories
The crossing of appearances
   rhymes and rebuses
      the hours of the fugue
   hounding humming
the school for conversation
   everyday things
      the darkness of the peaks
   the table the chair
the holidays of darkness
   jangling bells
      the conversation of statues
   for the carnival
the castle of hours
   tubas and drums
      the appearances of evening
   organs and whistles
   for parades
   bottles and glasses
   the apple and the pear
   the leaf and the bird
   curtains and windows
The arts of the fugue
   plaster casts
      the evening of shadows
   of antique statues

Je veux vous surprendre
en utilisant
les mots les plus simples
souvenirs d'école
La traversée des apparences
   rébus et comptines
      les heures de la fugue
   fredons tarabustes
l'école de la conversation
   objets quotidiens
      les ténèbres des cimes
   la table et la chaise
les vacances des ténèbres
   crécelles grelots
      la conversation des statues
   pour le carnaval
le château des heures
   tubas et tambours
      les apparences du soir
   orgues et sifflets
   pour les défilés
   bouteilles et verres
   la pomme et la poire
   la feuille et l'oiseau
   rideaux et fenêtres
Les arts de la fugue
   les copies en plâtre
      le soir des ombres
   des statues antiques

the call of the peaks
to sketch them
the statues of flame
in art classes
the future of statues
and for the older ones
the peaks of morning
the female nude
the signs of evening
in studios
the fugues of summer
the fields of Flanders
with their orchards
sheer mountains
far-distant lands
without vegetation
the seaside
The star of the shadows
the quiet outskirts
the summer of sighs
of rainy towns
the flames rekindled
and the clerks
the morning of errors
of businesses banks
the promises of morning
in their hats
the flames of grandeur
growing in number

l'appel des cimes
pour les dessiner
les statues des flammes
dans les classes d'art
l'avenir des statues
et pour les plus grands
les cimes du matin
le nu féminin
les signes du soir
dans les ateliers
les fugues d'été
les plaines des Flandres
avec leurs vergers
montagnes abruptes
des pays lointains
sans végétation
le bord de la mer
L'étoile des ombres
les faubourgs tranquilles
l'été des soupirs
des villes pluvieuses
le retour des flammes
et les employés
le matin des erreurs
d'entreprises banques
les promesses du matin
avec leurs chapeaux
les flammes des grandeurs
se multipliant

the adventures of summer
till they fill
the shadows of the fields
the entire sky
easels mirrors
my dear devotees
to set you free
and set them free
I shall trigger
The bridge of sighs
a sneeze
the field of appearances
in your gaze
the museum of errors
by displacing
the grandeur of conversation
by turning round
delusions of grandeur
by overturning
the errors of darkness
by doubling
the key to the fields
dazzling them
the sighs of the hours
to edge our way
with the wink of an eye
into the paradise
of prankster children

les aventures de l'été
jusqu'à envahir
les ombres des champs
le ciel tout entier
chevalets miroirs
mes chers amateurs
pour vous délivrer
et les délivrer
je vais provoquer
Le pont des soupirs
un éternuement
le champ des apparences
dans votre regard
le musée des erreurs
par déplacement
les grandeurs de la conversation
par retournement
la folie des grandeurs
par renversement
les erreurs des ténèbres
par dédoublement
la clef des champs
les éblouissant
les soupirs des heures
pour nous faufiler
avec un clin d'œil
dans le paradis
des enfants farceurs

The False Mirror (*Le Faux Miroir*), ca. 1950. Oil on canvas, 24 x 32 cm. Private collection

Daniel Abadie

The Unclassifiable Painting of René Magritte

There are works of art that seem to be perfectly closed in on themselves: they are so singular, in their workmanship as in everything else, that they invite neither parallels nor comparisons. This is the case with the painting of René Magritte. Even to link it with the work of the Surrealists is to cordon it off. In the context of the Surrealist movement, it has less in common with the technical innovators—the collages or frottages of Max Ernst, automatic writing, Masson's sand paintings or Miró's color planes, to name but a few—than with the practices of the far less numerous painters of images (Dalí, Tanguy), all of whose work can be traced back to the world of De Chirico. But even then, although Tanguy, and to a greater extent Dalí, attempt to fix on the canvas the unpredictable images of dreams, to render visible the dark night of consciousness, Magritte is more faithful than they to the lessons of De Chirico; he concentrates on *enigma*,[1] in an attempt to represent mystery in broad daylight.

The incongruous relationships between two objects appearing in the paintings of Magritte—an apple and a face, a shoe and a foot, a glass and a cloud; or between two qualities—a person in stone, a trombone in flames; or between two orders—clouds becoming birds or figures turning into wood—are not intended to refer to the imagery of dreams (since this, by its very nature, explains and justifies everything), but rather to suggest

a mysterious order "which forbids thought from being satisfied by any of the questions that might be asked, or by any of the answers that might be found to these questions."[2] Strangely enough (for a *Surrealist*), Magritte's work starts with a methodical scrutiny of reality. As in Cartesian philosophy, everything suddenly becomes the subject of fundamental doubt— a face is hollow and conceals an abyss, day coexists with night, a rock defies gravity and rises up into the air, bearing a fortress on its crest[3]—for, as the title of one of his paintings tells us, what the painter is representing is "the universe unmasked" (*L'Univers démasqué*, 1932).

With something of the detached outlook of a scientist,[4] Magritte reproduces his mysteries in exactly the condition in which they appear to him, but he introduces into them, in experimental fashion, readings which allow us to investigate the very nature of the phenomenon. So, for example, the mermaid may have retained her legs, but the upper half of her body is replaced by the head and body of a fish; the cracked, irregular crust of a bread roll bears the jagged relief pattern of the earth's crust, with a range of mountains silhouetted against the horizon. There is no apparent symbolism attached to the objects depicted: Magritte states explicitly that "to my eyes, my paintings are valid if the objects they represent resist being interpreted in terms of symbols, or being explained by any other means."[5]

One may justifiably wonder, nevertheless, what psychological deformity in the viewers' nature (if we are to believe Magritte) could possibly lead them to see images with strong sexual connotations in some of the objects depicted by the artist. The potential symbolic interpretation of a pipe, a cowbell or a candle could be just the outcome of an obsessional need to analyze— given the deliberately straightforward way in which they are painted. In one painting, however, *Irène or The Forbidden Reading* (*Irène ou La Lecture défendue*), the artist's (occasional) connivance is made perfectly clear in the title: if the first name belongs to Irène Hamoir, the wife of Scutenaire, it was also the name used in the title

---

1 The word appears in most of the titles of De Chirico's earliest metaphysical paintings: *The Enigma of the Oracle* (1909), *The Enigma of an Autumn Afternoon* (1909), *The Enigma of Time* (1910-11), *The Enigma of Arrival and the Afternoon* (1911-12), etc.

2 Magritte, letter to André Bosmans, December 1963, in *Ecrits complets* (Paris: Flammarion, 1979).

3 Although Magritte rejected all attempts to explain his images, one cannot help noticing that popular speech contains certain expressions which suggest some of the painter's images: "*ce type est complètement creux, c'est un abîme de bêtise*" ("that fellow is hollow to the core, he's an abyss of stupidity") or "*c'est sans gravité*" ("that carries no weight").

4 In *La Ligne de vie*, a lecture given by Magritte in 1938 at the Koninklijk Museum voor Schone Kunsten in Antwerp, he stressed that: "this detached manner of depicting objects seems to me to come from a universal style, in which the likes and dislikes of the individual no longer play any part."

5 Georges d'Amphoux, "Conversation avec un surréaliste: les idées de Magritte," in *Ecrits complets* (Paris: Flammarion, 1979).

of an admirable book published clandestinely and anonymously by Aragon in 1928, *Le Con d'Irène* (Irène's Pussy), and the finger pointing towards the slit in the bell leaves us in no doubt about the meaning of this "forbidden" reading.

During the post-war period, when the spread of abstraction among the avant-garde seemed to have relegated all figurative painting to the past, Magritte's cool view of reality and its most banal elements (bread, apple, rose, umbrella, bowler hat, etc.) seemed even more extraordinary because his academic, impersonal style emphasized his desire to detach himself from representation, or to make representation into a simple statement about the strangeness of every actual object when considered on its own merits.

Although Magritte had initially used this desire for neutrality in both perception and treatment to cause surprise, it was to become the motive force behind the first wave of American Pop artists, who in the early 1960s were reacting against the trivialization of abstract painting. What might appear to be nothing more than an arbitrary relationship or a chance encounter is validated by the familiarity of New York with the artist's work (fifteen one-man shows—including a retrospective at the Museum of Modern Art in 1965—were held in the city before Magritte's death in 1967), and by the fact that Robert Rauschenberg and Jasper Johns both acquired paintings by him for their private collections. With regards to Pop art, a number of Magritte's paintings have a decidedly prophetic feel. The three hundred dollar bills depicted so meticulously, yet without any narrative thrust, in *The Fissure* (*La Fissure*, 1949) cannot fail to remind us of the use of banknotes in Warhol's paintings of 1962; similarly, the figures repeated regularly over the surface of the painting of a man in a bowler hat in *Golconda* (*Golconde*, 1953) and the bread rolls swarming over the sky like a flotilla of spaceships in *The Golden Legend* (*La Légende dorée*, 1958) seem to prefigure the systematic repetition of motifs by the American artist in his "wallpapers."[6]

During an exhibition in 1963 of the work of Jim Dine at the Galerie Aujourd'hui in Brussels, in which the work *Hat*[7] was on show, Marcel Broodthaers wrote about "the large paintings with a shelf, a bit like a mantel": "one

of these depicts a bowler hat and—stroke of genius— on the shelf are a real melon and a hat [*chapeau melon* is French for bowler hat—Trans.]. Well, not entirely, in fact, for it is covered with a layer of (black) paint which seems to stick to it.... All Magritte's paintings are famous in New York. Magritte is famous. He remains loyal to his early preferences, while continuing to develop a poetic language designed to undermine the normal language by which we live. The life-sized bowler hat by Jim Dine is, I imagine, intended as homage."[8]

Alterations of scale, a system frequently used by Magritte to remove the utilitarian aspect of an object, or to provide a new perception of it—how should one approach the comb the size of a wardrobe depicted in *Personal Values* (*Les Valeurs personnelles*, 1952), or avoid a new slant on the feather the size of a tower in *Night in Pisa* (*La Nuit de Pise*, 1953)?—recall the bewilderment

Claes Oldenburg, *Bath Tub, Hard Model*, 1966, 207 x 84 x 87 cm, Museum Ludwig, Cologne

6 For example the wallpapers *Cow* (1966) and *Mao* (1974).
7 *Hat*, 1961, 164 x 142 cm, Ileana Sonnabend Collection, New York.
8 Marcel Broodthaers, "Gare au défi," *Journal des Beaux-Arts*, Brussels, 14 November 1963.

caused by the colossal scale of Claes Oldenburg's oversized sculptures. In addition to enlargement, Oldenburg seems also to have been inspired by Magritte's early investigations into the nature of objects.[9] The numerous *petrification* paintings of the 1950s convey an impression of systematic research. And is not the *Bath Tub* (1966) made of corrugated cardboard—one of Oldenburg's few "hard" works—the exact antithesis of the lighted stone candle whose flame could never melt the material it is made from in Magritte's *Memory of a Journey* (*Souvenir de voyage*, 1955)? Normal use would soon give this object the same flabby texture characterizing Oldenburg's other sculptures. Although the idea of soft structures, such a distinctive feature of the artist's work, derives directly from the work of Dalí, Oldenburg certainly found food for thought in Magritte's work on such matters as scale and the alteration of the intrinsic qualities of the object.

Similarly, the reversed viewpoint in Magritte's *Atlantis* (*L'Atlantide*, 1927), in which the painted architecture of the staircase in the upper left-hand corner only makes sense when looked at upside down, as if the spectator were considering the reflection in the painted bathtub in the lower part of the painting, gives a foretaste of the viewpoint ordained by the three-dimensional transformation in Oldenburg's *Bedroom Ensemble*,[10] or James Rosenquist's repeated use of upside-down images in his paintings, suggesting contradictory ways of reading the work.

As with Oldenburg, but this time in painting, the work of Domenico Gnoli, whose years of major creativity coincided with his arrival in New York, is indebted to the work of Magritte: not only in the emphasis given to enlarged objects, but also in the artist's ability to remove the objects from their normal context in order to give them a new prominence. The shirt collar, the parting in the hair, the knot in the tie— each enlarged to fill a whole wall—are variations featuring everyday objects on the idea of *The Treachery of Images* (*La Trahison des images*), Magritte's celebrated pipe, painted against a neutral background like a road sign.[11] Gnoli could certainly have appropriated the description given by Magritte of his own work: "The means employed by M. to display objects consists

---

9 The lignification of the character in Magritte's *Discovery* (*Découverte*), dates from 1927.
10 *Bedroom Ensemble*, 1969, 518 x 640 cm, Whitney Museum, New York.
11 Can it be fortuitous that Harry Torczyner, the collector, friend and exegete of Magritte, also possessed two of Gnoli's major paintings?

Atlantis (*L'Atlantide*), 1957–8. Gouache on paper, 23.3 x 17.3 cm. Private collection, courtesy Timothy Baum, New York

Domenico Gnoli, *Hair Part*, 1968. Oil on canvas, 121 x 150 cm, Staatsgalerie moderner Kunst, Munich

of ridding them rigorously of their utilitarian aspects; presented thus, they gain the ability to seem absolutely useless and unusable, they become enigmas, eluding any scientific explanation."[12]

Of all the artists of the Pop art generation whose work displays links with Magritte's oeuvre, no one absorbed his influence as fully as Jasper Johns. The attention paid by Johns to the work of Duchamp, in particular to the *Large Glass*, had the effect of partially concealing the depth of his study of art history (Pop artists are not generally credited with this interest), and of his desire to situate the spirit of his work within the continuum of the avant-garde movements of the twentieth century. Much as the heritage of Cubism was essential to the formation of Johns's pictorial language (in particular the version of the Delaunays, who in the 1920s painted targets, used wax paint and stenciled lettering), Magritte's impact was certainly greater than that of any other Surrealist artist, and was of crucial importance to Johns's conceptual approach. Johns's choice of *The Interpretation of Dreams* (*La Clef des songes*, 1935) to represent Magritte in his collection is highly significant. In this painting, evidently influenced by the memory of old illustrated spelling books, each of the four images is accompanied by a supposedly descriptive caption. Under the picture of a horse is written: *the door*; under a clock: *the wind*; a pitcher is captioned: *the bird*; and only the picture of a valise is correctly captioned: *the valise*.

The subtle variations Johns produced using the names of colors (mainly the three primary colors, perhaps implicitly answering the question posed by Barnett Newman in that icon of American abstract painting *Who is Afraid of Red, Yellow and Blue? I*)[13] are most strikingly developed in the pseudo-improvised color wash of *False Start* (1959). Using the Cubist device of stenciled letters, Johns painstakingly names the colors, thereby demonstrating the limitations of both verbal and pictorial language and the impossible way they overlap. The words *red*, *yellow* and *blue* may be painted in the colors they designate, on a background of another color (for example, the word *blue* written in blue letters on an orange ground) or vice versa (*blue* in yellow letters on a blue ground), while the name and the color patch may also be free of any association (*blue* in orange letters

The Interpretation of Dreams (*La Clef des songes*), 1952. Gouache on paper, 19.1 x 14.3 cm. Timothy Baum Collection, New York

Jasper Johns, *False Start*, 1959. Oil on canvas, 170.8 x 137.2 cm. David Geffen Collection, Los Angeles

12 René Magritte, "La Peinture inutile de M.," in *Ecrits complets* (Paris: Flammarion, 1979).
13 *Who is Afraid of Red, Yellow and Blue? I*, 187.5 x 120 cm, S.I. Newhouse Collection, New York.

on a red ground). In *Jubilee* (1959),[14] a kind of pendant to *False Start* painted in grisaille, Johns replaced the colors by various shades of gray, thus emphasizing the highly speculative nature of this reflection on language: here the stenciled names of the colors are no more than mental references, a conceptual counterpoint to the pleasure of painting.

A painter stating, like Magritte, that he was not an artist but a man who thinks, was inevitably going to be held up as an example to those who, following Jasper Johns's pictorial lead, were to give conceptual art its theoretical dimension. It is clear that the concept, introduced by Joseph Kosuth in works such as his *One or Three Chairs* (1965),[15] of juxtaposing a real object with a photograph of that object, plus its dictionary definition, conforms closely to the principle established by Magritte in *The Treachery of Images* (although without involving the actual act of painting) and by Johns in *False Start*. But whereas Kosuth establishes a pattern of equivalences between the definition, the image and the object, Magritte (with Johns following his lead) creates a balancing act, sowing seeds of a "principle of doubt" in the mind of the viewer. By giving the image any number of possible interpretations, of which no single one can prevail, he provides a richness of layers of meaning which differs radically from the conceptual message.

The pipe in Magritte's painting is neither the reproduction of a physical object nor an idealized pipe, the Platonic model of the object "pipe". First and foremost it is a painting and thus, in this sense, "this is not a pipe." Thanks to the neutrality of the painting technique and the clarity of the message, however, the painted image unmistakably conveys a generic idea of the object. What might appear to be a Surrealist paradox—the image of a pipe negated by its caption, in the same fashion as Georg-Christoph Lichtenberg's paradox so dear to Breton: "a knife without a blade whose handle is missing"—turns out to be one of the most effective means ever invented of undermining language, visual or verbal.[16] At a lecture delivered in Charleroi in 1956, Camille Goemans rightly stated: "In fact, in this painting, by a brilliant trick which one might term the double absence of the object, in this case the pipe—absence in the representation, absence in the title—Magritte enforced the presence of this object in a truly mind-blowing manner.... [He] reduced the word and the image to a kind of common denominator and this common denominator was neither the canvas nor the painting but reality itself—something either on this side or on the far side of the picture, but implicating the picture and implicating us as well."[17]

Of all the artists potentially influenced by the lessons of Magritte, it was of course Marcel Broodthaers who was best placed to take heed. To an artist who had made mussels, coal and the colors of the Belgian flag the distinguishing features of his work, Magritte's "*Belgitude*" or "Belgian-ness," referred to so often in his letters,[18] appeared the merest wink—a wink made more ironic by the fact that the Surrealists as a group tirelessly proclaimed the internationalism of the movement. For a poet like Broodthaers, Magritte's relationship with language—so pronounced among the painters of his generation[19]—opened the way to a "predictable" type

14 *Jubilee*, 1959, 152.4 x 111.8 cm, Michael and Judy Ovitz Collection, Los Angeles.

15 *One or Three Chairs*, 1965, Centre Georges Pompidou, Musée National d'Art Moderne, Paris.

16 I am grateful to Pierre Alechinsky for the following information about the nature of the pipe: Christian Dotremont pointed out to him that the word *Ceci* could not refer to the pipe under any circumstances (it is masculine and the word *pipe* is feminine), and this remark was borne out by the plan for a logogram: "*Ceci* est un logogramme". In his essay on the relationship between Magritte and Broodthaers (in the exhibition catalogue *Magritte en compagnie*, Brussels 1997), Thierry de Duve returns to this matter and investigates it at great length.

17 Camille Goemans, *Œuvre* (Brussels: André de Rache, 1970).

18 For example in his letters to Louis Scutenaire. See pp. 266ff in this catalogue.

19 Worth noting is the fact that although a number of artists connected with Surrealism—from Max Ernst to Masson, from Dalí to Bellmer—left a considerable body of literary work, none of them, with the exception of Miró and Magritte, sought to make the connection between writing and painting.

Marcel Broodthaers, *Thighbone of a Belgian*, ca. 1964-5. Painted bone, 8 x 47 x 10 cm. Private collection

Jean-Marc Bustamante, *The Christmas Trees*, 1994–6. Steel, anti-corrosive paint, varnish, concrete; tree: 230 x 48 x 1 cm; socle: 15 x 60 x 20 cm. Private collection

of expression, of an apparently heterogeneous nature. In Magritte, and particularly in what appeared to be the sidelines of the artist's creative activity (photography, films, etc.), Broodthaers discovered more than just the painter with the academic technique, venerated in his own country. He detected signs of a libertarian attitude towards the means of creation, and an effort to produce work which escaped from the traditional forms of expression to attain a higher state of consciousness.

Direct references to Magritte in the work of Broodthaers are frequent after 1963, the year in which he executed his first works in the domain of the visual arts: *La Malédiction de Magritte (Les Nuages)* (*The Malediction of Magritte* [*The Clouds*]), 1966, *Magritte* (silk-screen print, 1967), *Rue René Magritte Straat* (1968), *Ceci ne serait pas une pipe* (*This Would not Seem to Be a Pipe*; film produced between 1968 and 1970). On the invitation to the exhibition at the Galerie Aujourd'hui in 1965, Broodthaers himself wrote: "I have only followed in the footprints left in the artistic sand by René Magritte and Marcel Duchamp, and the fresher footsteps of George Segal, Roy Lichtenstein and Claes Oldenburg."

It would be wearisome to name all the artists who, since 1970, have made reference to the spirit and

methods of Magritte in their work,[20] for, as Scutenaire noted ironically in his *Inscriptions*, "The Surrealists spawned some pretty terrible offspring." In a period when quotation has become a constant component of works of art, references vary from direct allusion, as in *The Christmas Trees* by Jean-Marc Bustamante, whose silhouettes in cut-out metal look like the three-dimensional embodiment of the cut-out figures in *The Finery of the Storm* (*La Parure de l'orage*, 1927), to the transposition of a whole system to another medium: the juxtaposition of four identical images which forms the composition of *The Man with the Newspaper* (*L'Homme au journal*, 1928) prefigures the sequential principle used in Duane Michals's photographs of Magritte. Michals's interest in Magritte was so great that he made several photographic portraits of the artist (an unprecedented phenomenon in his work).

However, it is the sudden, brutal break in the apparently well-established continuity of Magritte's work in 1943 that seems to have caught the imagination of the younger generation of painters since 1980: with unsuspected versatility, Magritte launched himself first into his "Renoir" period, then for a brief spell in 1948 into his "Vache" period (which ended in the failure of the exhibition of these paintings at the Galerie du Faubourg, Paris). The deliberate break with every identifying feature of his work, and his refusal to be assimilated into any style have become major sources of inspiration in modern art—since it rejected the academic tradition and gave pride of place to the inventiveness of the individual artist. Until the 1970s, most painters handled the problem by allowing forms to evolve gradually; their concern to present a coherent body of work led them to move from period to period in styles that fitted together harmoniously. It was not until an artist such as Gerhard Richter entered the scene that rejection of style became an aesthetic and moral stand: from one series of paintings to another, Richter juxtaposes photographic realism in monochrome, the gestural brushwork of his *Stadtbilder* and the conceptual character of his photographic *Atlas*. As Benjamin Buchloh observes: "Rather than constantly talking of a painting as something successfully achieved, once and for all, it might be better if critics reflected on the failed aspects of the painting, contributing thus towards turning reality and its discourse into possible new sources of success.... The painting of Gerhard Richter seems to provoke a similar misapprehension of epistemological scepticism. Worse still, the apparent

20 An attempt was made, for the Walloon artists, in the exhibition *Magritte en compagnie*, Centre culturel de la Communauté française Le Botanique, Brussels, 1997.

complexity and contradictions (plus the genuine dialectic) of the formal technique in Richter's work seem to be based on his own epistemological scruples: the fact that reality does not allow itself to be recognized. If recognition should take place, it is only through disparate fragments, via a deliberate inconsistency of perspective and the non-congruence of the facts recognized."[21]

Although Picasso remains a prime example of this approach, because of his weathervane temperament, his continual innovation and his ability to entertain antithetical points of view, artists since Richter wishing to create a contemporary style from the absence of style have looked more towards artists like Picabia and Magritte, preferring the deliberate nature of their breaks with style and their taste for mockery. During Magritte's "Vache" period,[22] the artist's challenging attitude towards his former academic style, plus the deliberately wooden style of painting and strident colors he adopted, displayed a disregard of the idea of art which was not

present in the impressionist luminosity of the paintings of the "Renoir" period, with their cloying sensuality. Nevertheless, the two series, so different in appearance, were born of the same profound sense of revolt. Rejection of a world dominated for five years by war, rejection of the deliberate obfuscations of Surrealism promoted by Breton, scorn for the social pretensions of poets and artists, disappointment with the lack of interest in his work beyond his small circle of friends: his aim to establish "sunlit Surrealism" during the "Renoir" period transgressed the rules of the avant-garde dialectically just as much as the "Vache" period transgressed them violently. During the latter, the example of the new abstract paintings by Picabia (with whom Magritte resumed friendly relations in 1946) was crucial. As Magritte wrote at the time: "The paintings of Picabia should not make us dream of the 'revelations' to be gleaned from coffee dregs, or 'prophesies' that require too much patience to verify. Picabia thinks as we should all think. In 1946 he contrasts an overwhelming past with movement and flashes of bright light which reveal life in all its grandiose isolation."[23]

For Magritte, at whatever time he was working, and whatever style or technique he was adopting, the main thing (and what he so rightly admired in Picabia) was to *escape from fixed ideas*. Although painting fixes things and images, what Magritte wanted most of all to render was the permanent movement of the mind which nothing can ever immobilize, no definition can prove satisfying and, if "this continues not to be a pipe,"[24] it is because the reality of the world remains, whatever anyone may do, the great unclassifiable mystery.

---

21 Benjamin Buchloh, "Ready-made, photographie et peinture dans la peinture de Gerhard Richter," in *Gerhard Richter* (Paris: Editions du Centre Georges Pompidou, 1977).

22 Although this name harks back ironically to the term "Fauve" (which explains the sudden emphasis on color in these paintings), it is also possible that it should be seen as a *vacherie* (dirty trick) at the expense of Paul Delvaux, Magritte's rival for the favors of Belgian collectors. To Mesens, who introduces the name of Delvaux several times into a study of Magritte, Magritte wrote in 1946: "*Encore du veau!* ["More veal!": a pun on the name Delvaux. —Trans.] I propose to serve beef or cow."

23 René Magritte, "Francis Picabia, la peinture animée," in *Ecrits complets* (Paris: Flammarion, 1979).

24 The phrase figures in several of Magritte's drawings; the first version was published in the review *Temps mêlés* in 1952.

The Treachery of Images (*La Trahison des images*), 1952.
Chinese ink on paper, 19 x 27 cm. Private collection

The Musings of a Solitary Walker (*Les Rêveries du promeneur solitaire*), 1926. Oil on canvas, 139 x 105 cm.
Private collection, Belgium

Jean Roudaut

A Grand Illusion

Illusion: the action, or an act, of deceiving the bodily eye by false or unreal appearances, or the mental eye by false prospects, statements, etc.—The fact or condition of being deceived or deluded by appearances, or an instance of this; a mental state involving the attribution of reality to what is unreal.
—*The Oxford English Dictionary*

Surrealist painting, especially that of Magritte, has been called literary. Several reasons may be suggested for this assessment. In moving past those styles of painting that were investigating new forms of illusion (Impressionism, Cubism) to pick up the thread of the *trompe-l'œil* technique, Magritte's painting almost seems to present a blueprint of reality where, like the image of reality we summon up in our mind's eye, what is real is clear and distinct. Magritte's works respect Cartesian dioptrics. And yet, the originality of their conception surprises us. They show us the world not as we were taught it is, but as it should become. Each painted object is recognizable and namable. The images are accurate and unequivocal, but their relationship to one another is enigmatic. If we apply the elements of rhetoric to Magritte's painting, the *inventio* (the search for motifs) and the equivalent of the *elocutio* (accuracy of drawing and trueness of color) remain classical, while the arrangement of the composition, the *dispositio*, seems mysterious.

Another, more important reason why Magritte's painting almost reads like a novel has to do with its allusions, which are mainly literary. Writers write in critical imitation of previous works, though often opposing them, out of admiration. Painters—Picasso revisiting Courbet, Bacon meditating on Velázquez—deal with works from the past just as much as writers do. But Magritte functions less readily through allusion to paintings (except when he cites David and Manet) than to Baudelaire and Poe. Because of this, he has been called an *imagier* (image maker) more often than a painter, because the word "image" is so close to the word "imagination."

Recall Arthur Gordon Pym's remark, in Chapter 25 of his travel account, upon the change in the nature of his surroundings as he progresses: "Many unusual phenomena now indicated that we were entering upon a region of novelty and wonder." This could serve as an epigram for Magritte's oeuvre, as epitomized in *The Enchanted Domain* at Knokke-le-Zoute. And ye who enter into his garden, lay down all hope of strolling in a reassuringly familiar space. When combined otherwise, our ways of representing the landscape to ourselves reveal its fecundity. Already present though still hidden here, a world begins to unfold; the paintings foreshadow it and hasten its advent. Among the things that contribute to making this transformation effect noticeable are Magritte's care of composition and his original use of titles that evoke Baudelaire and Poe. An unusual and astonishing feat is performed so that human beings may one day sit at the table of the gods.

Cézanne's Compote

One of the simplest ways of disconcerting the viewer is to unhinge what is to be looked at from what is to be read, that is, the title or caption. Cézanne designated a dish filled with fruit by its usual name of "compotier." In 1925, Magritte quite traditionally called a picture of a female body in a bathing suit *Bather*. For complex mythological and religious works, titles aid in guiding interpretation. They enable the viewer to locate the depicted scene within the framework of a narrative and arouse an awareness of the gap between what is shown through shapes and colors and what is said in words. The critical distance linking a painting to its title is the same as that linking the painting, along with its title, to its pictorial or literary references. In 1950, when Magritte called a painting of a right-angled coffin *David's Madame Récamier*, the title took on the function of an annotation: (a) the painting does not evoke a person but her representation by David; (b) what is enclosed within the wooden planks would be Mme. Récamier neither as she was (when alive) nor as she has become (a skeleton), but as what she was promised she would be. Magritte's painting reveals the ineluctable; it completes David's. This title is on a par with the caption *This Is Not a Pipe* (*Ceci n'est pas une pipe*). That image from 1929, although true to one's idea of what a pipe looks like, is not an object you can pick up in your hands. In the same vein, a 1964 title alerts the viewer that *This Is Not an Apple* (*Ceci n'est pas une pomme*). The painted apple cannot be bitten into any more than the bowl of the painted pipe can be lit. The title emphasizes the fact that to call a representation of apples "apples" is not only equivocal but a fallacy. It is not things that are represented, but a vision of things. A representation dispossesses an object of its being. Thus, in presenting to view an image or a "perspective," a representation is of interest only for what it is not.

While the titles of most paintings are naively redundant, Magritte's titles seem to challenge representation, without, however, being alien to it. The title *The Difficult Crossing* (*La Traversée difficile*, 1926) evokes a part of what is represented—two sailing ships caught in a storm can be seen, either on a canvas hung on the far wall of the room or through a huge window open onto nature's fury. This "picture within a picture" may be ascribed an allegorical value (existence as a perilous voyage). The title may also be taken as a key to the utterly heteroclite surroundings of the central painting in its "host": a plaster hand lying on a table with one human leg, a tall, thin post with an open eye, sheets of plywood with cut-out holes. *The Birth of the Idol* (*La Naissance de l'idole*, 1926) juxtaposes similarly disparate elements: the image of a raging sea behind a post like the markers used to cordon off a danger zone (its femininity is expressed by a hand). Standing on a male dummy (a sort of shooting gallery target), the idol (originally, the word simply denoted an image) towers over the waves and defies the dark sky. Magritte's titles quite consistently have a value that is both self-reflexive (the birth of the idol refers to the composition of the image) and figurative: the difficult crossing (we are all in the same boat) does not take place amid the maelstrom and thunder crash of events, but amid the signs and images that are our reality. The elements of anxiety (night, sea) and signs of triumph (an idol that scoffs at danger) must be combined. Another title from the same period, *The Secret Player* (*Le Joueur secret*, 1927), could make you think the work is meant as a rebus. Where is the secret player hidden? Is it the gloved athlete in the center, watching the game being played with a bat or, in the open booth, the woman gagged by the mask she wears? Or the turtle-like object? Despite its obvious heaviness, it floats through the air; it is black, as is appropriate for a turtle, an animal whose name means "of Tartarus, hell, the world of shades." We play our whole life long with death at work surreptitiously within us. It appears to us only through anamorphosis; we avoid going out of our way mentally to see it. Magritte's paintings may be thought of as metaphorical images. They do not transcribe our idea of reality: they expose the enigmatical aspect of what goes without saying.

While these titles engage in a dialogue with their respective paintings, there are others where, in an entirely original fashion, the caption lies outside the frame, accompanying the picture with words. The handwriting is that of a grade school primer and the layout that of an illustration in a science textbook, where the words are like objects. In contemplating them, the viewer is obliged to transform abstract signs (the words read) into natural images (identical to what those of the objects would be), whereas our mental path usually leads in the opposite direction, converting paintings into words. In a brief essay from 1928 entitled *Les Mots et les images* (Words and Images), Magritte recalls that a representation of things is a simulacrum ("ghost, phantom, appearance") and more serious still, that words and things have no connection with each other. Therefore, everything could be given a different name and recombined in an original way. Ionesco's *Bald Soprano* and Tardieu's *Un mot pour un autre* (One Word for Another) have demonstrated that we understand each other just as well when we substitute one word for another as when we use words' conventional attributions. Meaning depends less on semantics than on syntax. If the syntax is sturdy enough, substituting one noun for another does not impede understanding; the presence of unexpected objects in a solidly constructed pictorial space does not make *The Anger of the Gods* (*La Colère des dieux*, 1960) any less intelligible. The disparity between title and picture tends to its greatest as the objects represented are set apart and in relation to each other. Horse and automobile communicate through the intermediary of verbal elements (horse, horsepower) and cultural elements: the horse galloping on the roof at the same speed as the car will not fall to the ground any more than Zeno's arrow. Theoretically, time is suspended.

Like poetry, painting admits the principle of substitution. The interpretation of dreams has accustomed us to establishing equivalences of meaning between the objects represented, or described. Everything being reducible to the circle and line (more than the cone and square of Cézanne's dictum), the shape of an object tells us more than its name, which neutralizes it. In 1927, Magritte entitled a painting *The Interpretation of Dreams* (*La Clef des songes*). Using a licit object to suggest a meaning that is disapproved of wards off censure: with *La Marmotte*, Watteau evoked the way in which the right application of a flageolet can bring satisfaction to animal sensibility. In 1943, in his so-called Renoir period, Magritte gave the title *The First Day* (*Le Premier Jour*; as if an inverse reminiscence of Courbet's *Origin of the World*) to a painting where a young man plays the fiddle: his music for a low-down dance raises a ballerina between his legs. Magritte generalizes a method of particular usage. He transcribes the language of dreams, or of birds, visually.

Magritte's choice of titles falls into different modes. There was a Cézanne period, where the work's title quite conventionally designated the objects pictured, as if image and name were two sides of the same coin (we never let go the idea of a necessary, natural connection between a name and what it designates). At another period, the titles seem motivated by a concern for displacement: *The Glass Key* (*La Clef de verre*, 1959) is an enormous boulder balanced on an Alpine ridge. There was a period when the titles referred to a reality from the realm of art, such as *David's Madame Récamier* (1950), or literature—*The Domain of Arnheim* (1938). And Poe was not the only literary stimulus: for *Philosophy in the Boudoir* (*La Philosophie dans le boudoir*, 1947) it was Sade; for *The Legend of the Centuries* (*La Légende des siècles*, 1950), Victor Hugo. A small wooden, rush-bottom chair at the summit of a monumental rocky seat evokes, with ironic admiration, the transformation of Guernsey into a throne. And then there was the "Vache" period (*Prince Charming* [*Le Prince charmant*, 1948] is a young cock summoned from his castle). This was no mere passing phase in his oeuvre; mockery, if not sarcasm, is exercised politically and morally in the caricatures and paintings; humor, which upsets the rational mind, is constantly at work.

Magritte explained his choice of titles on various occasions: "The relationship of title to painting is poetic, that is, it retains only certain of the objects'

characteristics, which the conscious mind normally ignores but sometimes senses, on the occasion of extraordinary events that reason has not managed to elucidate."[1] Every system of classification is based on the qualities that the associated objects have in common and discounts the individual characteristics of each. The link between the title and the work is not inconceivable, but is yet to be conceived. The exchange between text and image must make possible a project of consciousness. The painting's composition is governed by the idea that an object is the equivalent of a question (for nothing is taken for granted) to which a provisional answer is provided by another object. The painting associates them to compose an autonomous group; at a distance from it, inscribed in another writing system, the title in turn constitutes an autonomous object. The relationship of the title to the work is similar to the painting's essence, comprised of exchange and interference. This relationship may be expressed in a diagram patterned on the model de Saussure proposed for words:

Object A	Object B	
Painting		Verbal accompaniment

The painting is based on unremarked similarities between A and B. In the same way, a relationship of analogy is established with the title. Each refers to the other.

Magritte said that a painting does not illustrate its title. Neither does the title comment on it: it is an element of movement. Painting, like every other form of thought, must contribute to the changing of society and the maturation of the human race. The caption nudges the work towards a future, other world that the painting and its title together foreshadow.

Magritte frequently selected titles from suggestions made by friends in the course of conversation. He chose simple expressions, often taken directly, or slightly altered, from literature: *The Musings of a Solitary Walker* (*Les Rêveries du promeneur solitaire*), *The Misanthropes* (*Les Misanthropes*), *The Golden Legend* (*La Légende dorée*), *Almayer's Folly* (*La Folie Almayer*) and so forth.

---

1 René Magritte, *Écrits complets*, ed. André Blavier (Paris: Flammarion, 2001), "Sur les titres," no. 68, p. 259.

Baudelaire and Poe

The paintings evoke Rousseau, Voragine and Conrad, but not as constantly or intensely as Baudelaire and Poe. Michel Butor, writing about words in painting and what they mean (*Les mots dans la peinture*, Skira, 1969), suggested that the source of *The Art of Conversation* (*L'Art de la conversation*, 1950) was a verse from Baudelaire, the opening of Poem XVII from the *Flowers of Evil* entitled "Beauty": "I am as lovely as a dream in stone." According to Butor, Magritte's work is a "conversation" between the painter and Baudelaire. They began talking well before 1950. Already in 1931, a painting entitled *The Giantess* (*La Géante*) recalls Poem XIX from the *Flowers of Evil*. Reduced in his imagination to the size of a child, the poet proclaims his desire to nestle in the hollow bend of a giant woman's leg and "To feel at leisure her stupendous shapes;/Crawl on the cliffs of her enormous knees."

Magritte's painting retains the disproportion evoked in Baudelaire's poem: the naked woman is taller than the door of the closed empty room, while the man, dressed in a suit, does not come up to the wainscoting. But with the man seen from behind and the woman facing the viewer, no contact between the two is foreseeable. So, whereas the poem suggests—beyond the complicity of the two bodies—a fusion of being and nature through the intermediary of a mother figure, this notion of communion is visually absent from the painting. The shift is partly glossed in the side panel to the right, where Magritte penned a sonnet he in turn entitled "The Giantess" and signed "Baudelaire." A variation on Baudelaire's sonnet, Magritte's is even less regular than the original. None of the first quatrain is from Baudelaire; the second stanza borrows some elements, though no complete lines. The two texts simply echo each other. Baudelaire's, present in memory, superimposes itself on the one being read. The reader senses a resemblance but reads a difference. Magritte alters the poem's tone, substituting affection for languor ("tenderly" in place of "at ease") and eternity for duration ("at leisure" becomes "forever"). To the experience of the senses, he prefers the renunciation of self. The changes are so considerable one might well wonder why, other than for aesthetic reasons, Magritte felt compelled to rely on Baudelaire's poem at all and, even more, why he wanted to involve the viewer's hypothetical memory of it. Two reasons come to mind. First, to create the impression of a modified repetition in the observer's mind, to awaken an uncanny feeling of similarity that the viewer must elucidate. As soon as the viewer notices a resemblance, he enters a kind of echo corridor, like those Magritte was fond of illustrating. Therein might lie the second reason for Magritte's conspicuous reliance on a previous work: deriving inspiration from David or Baudelaire does not mean imitating them, but carrying out one of their virtualities by repeating them. The readily discernible resemblances and disconcerting differences lead to an understanding of what had remained secret in Baudelaire's poem; in altering it, the painter carried it further. Accentuating the Baudelairian connection of desire and death, Magritte exposes what is lethal in the desire for maternal, and sensual, protection.

In 1931, Magritte was thirty-two years old. Like Dante, who at the beginning of *The Divine Comedy* thinks of himself as "*nel mezzo del cammin di nostra vita*," he considers he has the right to say he is "*au milieu de ma vie*" (midway in my life's journey), just when everything is reflected. But "*au milieu de ma vie*" could also mean at its core. *The Giantess*'s nature is different from that of the woman addressed by the poet-painter: she is what cannot be grasped, yet no more dissipates than mist on a river. Although she may have been known in a distant past, in the present she haunts the thought constantly weighing on the man in business attire with his back to the viewer. Here, returning to her —as Baudelaire, for whom the giantess represents the body of maternal nature, so strongly desires— would mean to die. We must stick to the world we are in, "base but of alluring grace." The lover saves the man from the woman made gigantic by her absence.

The connection between Baudelaire and Magritte is not restricted to a single poem. The coincidence of their literary and pictorial worlds is frequent and discreet. *Homesickness* (*Le Mal du pays*, 1941), for example, is felt by two figures: a winged man (his tailcoat changed into ancient plumage) and a lion "from proud Africa." We hover between spleen and the ideal. From Baudelaire's world, Magritte passed quite easily to the contiguous world of Poe.

Magritte called a painting from 1938 *The Domain of Arnheim* (*Le Domaine d'Arnheim*). The glaciers and eternal snows seen beyond a window ledge with two eggs resting on it could illustrate a page from Kant on the sublime: the scene is alluring and terrifying. According to what Magritte wrote in *La Ligne de vie* (Lifeline, 1938), his *Domain of Arnheim* "creates a vision that Edgar Allan Poe would have liked very much: it is a huge mountain

The Giantess (*La Géante*), 1931. Oil on canvas, gouache and Chinese ink on Isorel, 54 x 73 cm. Museum Ludwig, Cologne

whose shape coincides exactly with that of an eagle with outstretched wings."[2] The visual relationship of the egg and the bird, frequent in Magritte's oeuvre, suggests that something is hatching, a birth. The eagle is an image of excellence, arrived at through the recognition of the *genius loci*; it is likewise a sign of sovereignty. The image reveals the significance of raw matter. Thus, these are the marks of a "creation." However, although the painting's title is taken from one of Poe's tales (translated by Baudelaire), and despite what Magritte may say of the matter, Poe's world and his are different. According to Mr. Ellison, owner of the

Domain of Arnheim in Poe's tale, perfection of composition does not exist in nature but is only the result of art. Preserved for man, a being having become mortal through his own fault, the world that has survived is imperfect. It has the fragility and the weakness of something that is defective. Modern art must compensate for this deficiency and take as its goal "the creation of novel moods of purely physical loveliness."[3] In Arnheim, Ellison discovers a territory worth transforming into a visual and sensual paradise.

According to Poe's description, the domain is surrounded by rolling hills; a river serves as its highway; the valley is luxuriant with vegetation and flowers—it is the perfect image of an orchard. But Magritte replaces this fertility with ice and cold. He eliminates two marks from Poe's scene: the navigable river and the richly abundant plant life. "The chiselled stone has the hue of ages and is profusely

2 *Ibid.*, no. 42, p. 111. Quoted in English from *René Magritte. Catalogue raisonné*, ed. David Sylvester, vol. 2 (Houston: Menil Foundation/ Antwerp: Fonds Mercator, 1993), p. 262.
3 "The Domain of Arnheim," in *The Collected Works of Edgar Allan Poe*, ed. Thomas Ollive Mabbott, vol. 3 (Cambridge, Massachusetts: Belknap Press, 1978), p. 1271.

overhung and overspread with the ivy, the coral honeysuckle, the eglantine, and the clematis." Ellison mistrusts a vast panorama, for man is not happy except in seclusion. In fact, "In looking from the summit of a mountain we cannot help feeling abroad in the world. The heart-sick avoid distant prospects as a pestilence." True to this spirit, Magritte closes off his mountain landscape, precluding any lateral vista as well as any escape beyond the horizon: fleeing into the distance would be to evade one's condition. Indeed, the ruggedness of Magritte's landscape seems to be inspired by another of Poe's sketches, "Landor's Cottage, a Pendant to 'The Domain of Arnheim'." In it, the mountains are held to be the site of impulsive savagery, like the dark wood in Dante's time—a survival of original Chaos. Magritte preserves this inhuman impression by making the setting austere, signaled by the figure of the dominating carrion-eating eagle. The painter has excluded what would have indicated the possibility of living here and now, sensually, in nature, completely fulfilled as if by the intimacy of a giantess.

Baudelaire proposed the title "Habitations imaginaires" (Imaginary Dwellings) for three sketches Poe himself grouped together: "The Domain of Arnheim," "Landor's Cottage" and "The Philosophy of Furniture." Magritte keeps the spirit of a dwelling by giving his pictures a fictional framework. Yet he transforms the landscape: in *The Domain of Arnheim*, the earth is petrified and the waters are frozen. Cultivated nature appears only in the background of the works. A river flows discretely among pines. However, "Running water is water destined to slow down, to become heavy," according to Gaston Bachelard in his study on Poe. "Only water can die, be still, and yet keep its reflections."[4] The mountain is made of frozen water. It is a sort of tomb. René Magritte was thirteen in 1912, when his mother, at the age of forty, threw herself into the Sambre. In *The Invention of Life* (L'Invention de la vie,

1928), an apparently living figure is placed facing a form veiled by a shroud like a phantom. The heads of *The Lovers* (Les Amants, 1928) are covered in cloth that clings to their invisible faces as if it were wet. What lies behind the living face is as much an enigma as what is hidden. Inside the skull, sleigh bells jingle. Appearances are concealed behind appearances. The figures in *The Invention of Life* are placed mirrorwise; one cannot tell where hidden life begins, where real life leaves off. It is likewise difficult to distinguish the point in the picture where the sensory world ends and its future becomes visible. Where, in other words, do we see what we know and where do we see that which haunts what we see? The sky was so clear and the river so transparent around Landor's Cottage "that where the true bank ended and where the mimic one commenced, it was a point of no little difficulty to determine."[5]

"I like Edgar Allan Poe," Magritte told Marcel Fryns in 1966. "He has always had a very great importance for me, given his singular poetic preoccupations. I sense in him a kindred spirit, with whom I am in complete harmony."[6] Two of Poe's writings played a particular role in Magritte's thinking: "The Philosophy of Composition" (published by Baudelaire together with his translation of "The Raven" and a preamble of his own under the title "La Genèse d'un poème"), stressing the role of composition, and "Eureka," evoking the finality of a carefully thought-out work.

The question of construction is obviously the painter's natural concern. André Gide emphasizes that "It is through composition that a painter gives depth to his canvas. Without composition a work of art can offer only superficial beauty."[7] The use of perspective enabled Magritte to give depth to representation, but also to lead thought beyond the foreseeable, giving depth in a further figurative sense. Yet another purpose must be ascribed to this endeavor: if a work shows no purposiveness, it remains a mechanical exercise.

The Art of Composition

According to tradition, top and bottom correspond. In "Landor's Cottage," the lake echoes the sky and the trout in it may be mistaken for flying fish: "It was almost impossible to believe that they were not absolutely suspended in the air."[8] When you conceive of the world as a self-reflecting whole, everything in the mirror is the equivalent of what one imagines to be reality. What is before also comes after; what surprises is ordinary. There are strange and eerie objects in some of Magritte's

4 Gaston Bachelard, *L'Eau et les Rêves. Essai sur l'imagination de la matière* (Paris: Librairie José Corti, 1947), pp. 66 and 92. Quoted in English from "Deep Waters—Dormant Waters—Dead Waters: 'Heavy Waters'" in Edgar Allan Poe's Reverie," in *Water and Dreams: An Essay on the Imagination of Matter*, trans. Edith R. Farrell (Dallas: Pegasus Foundation, 1983), pp. 46–7 and 66.

5 "Landor's Cottage," in Poe, *op. cit.* note 3, p. 1333.

6 Magritte, *op. cit.* note 1, no. 191, p. 619.

7 André Gide, *Journal* (Paris: Bibliothèque de la Pléiade, 1970), "Feuillets," 1921, p. 716. Quoted in English from *The Journals of André Gide*, trans. Justin O'Brien, vol. 2: 1914–1927 (New York: Knopf, 1948), "Detached Pages," 1921, p. 286.

8 Poe, *op. cit.* note 3, p. 1333.

Homesickness (*Le Mal du pays*), 1941. Oil on canvas, 100 x 81 cm.
Private collection, Belgium

Collective Invention (*L'Invention collective*), 1935. Oil on canvas, 73 x 116 cm. Private collection

works—baluster-like wooden posts with human faces, a black flying turtle, an inverse mermaid (*Collective Invention* [*L'Invention collective*], 1935), bombards with bulging eyes (*The Cicerone* [*Le Cicérone*], 1947), three enormous sleigh bells hovering above a prairie (*The Voice of the Air* [*La Voix des airs*], 1931). But basically, the forms are identifiably those of our daily experience; they recall the sea and mountains without picturesqueness and trees made of a single leaf, as in Max Ernst's heliogravure *Les Mœurs des feuilles* (1925), reused in *Histoires naturelles* (1926). Less common in painting, if we leave aside *vanitas* still lifes, are the depictions of candles (which burn down) and eggs (which break). But with Magritte, the fleeting is fixed: flame and wax are of stone. Magritte drew up a concise list of his favorite objects: "The egg and the cage, the door and the void, the rose and the dagger, the piano and the ring, the bed sheet and the moon, the squirrel and its floor."[9] To that

list, compiled in 1954, he appended another in 1967: "A hat, a sleigh bell, an apple, an easel, a bird, a street lamp, a brick wall, shoes, a three-piece suit. Only, the hat sometimes sits on top of an apple, the bird is made of stone, the shoes are feet and have toes."[10] The most important thing about the earlier list lies in the conjunction "and," which associates two objects of different families, mixing apples and oranges. In the second list, the keyword is the modest "only." Both terms accentuate what is unforeseeable in the joint representation of two distant objects. Thought does not fail to find a relationship between the extremely bizarre pairs; similarly, the painting's aim is to relate the "odds and ends" impression to a higher necessity. If the pictorial work were not strictly composed, it would risk lapsing into incoherence. Composition is to a picture what syntax is to a sentence: it makes it possible to endow the disparate with a necessary meaning.

Magritte wrote that in 1922, when Lecomte showed him a photograph of De Chirico's *Song of Love*, he "could not hold back his tears."[11] What freedom of expression did De Chirico's painting suddenly reveal? First of all,

9 Magritte, *op. cit.* note 1, no. 111, p. 395.
10 *Ibid.*, no. 204, p. 660.
11 *Ibid.*, no. 106, p. 367.

the possibility of associating disproportionate objects in a plausible space. In Magritte's work, we come upon roses and apples occupying a room's entire volume, a comb grown larger than a bed, a shaving brush overhanging the top of an armoire, a monumental stemmed glass. The proportion of objects is subject to the *Personal Values* (*Les Valeurs personnelles*, 1951–2) attached to them. We experience this phenomenon when we misplace something, and our mental idea of it obliterates all other presence, so far out of proportion does it grow in our confined space. Magritte combined this method with another, more personal approach—the graft, where what begins in one realm is completed in another. *The Red Model* (*Le Modèle rouge*, 1935) is doubtless the best-known example. The living flesh of a foot veers into worn leather; a long walk on hot coals makes the shoe as sensitive as flesh. An equally surprising effect is the transparency with

which opaque objects are endowed: a ship constituted of the sea (its element); a bird (light as air) made of the wind. Each object can be thought of as an emblem of the medium in which it moves. The opposite of this system of correlation is one of disjuncture, where the representation of an object is placed in contradiction to its purpose: a door, cut out so that only an embracing couple can pass through it, is ill suited for everyday use. An *Amorous Vista* (*Perspective amoureuse*, 1935) is offered up to desire. Lighter than air, granite gravitates in the air. Taken in the mountains, clear water presents no danger.

Seeing De Chirico's painting may have given Magritte still more meaningful encouragement: De Chirico assembled the unexpected objects that caught his attention in an architecture that is pure (clean lines, distinct shadows) and idealized (series of arcades, as in Ferrara). The place contains an antique head, a rubber glove and a green ball. These objects are

Personal Values (*Les Valeurs personnelles*), 1952. Oil on canvas, 80 x 100 cm.
Museum of Modern Art, San Francisco

juxtaposed in space without a spiral to hold them in line, without colors flitting from one to the other. "My painting," Magritte wrote to Guy Mertens in 1966, "is a thought that *sees* without naming what it sees. What it sees in an object is another, hidden object."[12] In an entirely level, evenly lit place, the painter groups the chosen objects in such a way that one becomes the meaningful equivalent of the other. Each serves to reveal the other.

His limited selection of objects is not only factitious (because they are reduced to the state of images), but also fetishistic, because they partake of magical spells. They would appear dispersed on the canvas and disparateness would seem to take over the painting, except that they are grouped together in a conventional and severe setting (the theatrical chamber) or observed through a window. They are disposed according to the rules of perspective, applied strictly and conspicuously. Painters have often found enjoyment in disrupting this imperative of realistic representation laid down in Alberti's *Trattato della pittura* (1511). As a depiction of space is not a reality but a construct, in order to make it appear improbable, one need only alter the convention by diverting lines that should converge or compounding the number of vanishing points. This creates images that are inconsistent with a single viewpoint; the beholder must choose between contemplating Holbein's Ambassadors and identifying the patch spread out at their feet. One view excludes the other; one may choose worldliness and culture over what one is loath to look at—the skull. Fragments of space represented within a picture can also be irreconcilable. Hogarth's print entitled *False Perspective* (1754) anticipates the constructions of M.C. Escher (*Other World*, 1947). Magritte operates similarly in *Carte Blanche* (*Le Blanc-Seing*, 1965). A horse and rider are passing amid the trees of a forest. Part of the horse is hidden—not by a tree as one would expect, but by space itself, in a way that the mind is unable to conceive but finds delight in perceiving. Against all reason, a tree that perspectival illusion plants in the background comes to the fore to become entangled with the horse's hind leg. The work seems to denounce the ordinary construction of space and conjure a new world. A mirror in a painting can render the space imaginarily deeper or dislocate it. When a beautiful woman, seen from behind, is looking

at herself in a mirror, this artifice increases the believability of the space represented. But the same means may be used to dispute its cohesion. The beholder of Manet's *A Bar at the Folies-Bergère* (1882) cannot position himself so that the diversity of reflections seems to belong to the same space. Magritte made peculiar use of the mirror. He leaves it empty in *The Birth of the Idol* (1926) and on the bedroom wall of *The Giantess* (1931). In the portrait of Edward James entitled *Not to Be Reproduced* (*La Reproduction interdite*, 1937), he presents a logical impossibility rationally: the figure seen from the back in a space that convention maintains to be real is also seen from behind in the mirror, as if he had delegated his double to pass through the looking-glass. On a shelf in front of the mirror is a book whose title is legible: the French edition of Poe's *Narrative of Arthur Gordon Pym*.

The essential role of perspective in the pictures' composition is emphasized by the recurrent images of the window ledge and the threshold. Two spaces are thus suggested: we locate ourselves virtually in one of them and imagine the other as a recollection, or an anticipation. An exchange occurs between these two spaces, like that between stage and audience, the site of the model and that of his image. Magritte returns various times to the indispensable connection between near and far, even entitling one of his works *In Praise of the Dialectic* (*Eloge de la dialectique*, 1937). A window in the façade of a building opens onto a room whose back wall is a façade just like the first one. The title of the work, and its construction, are emblematic of the whole: not only individual objects, but spaces themselves take part in the exchange. No element holds the meaning of the whole; no appearance takes precedence over another.

As if to underline his interest in the traditional construction of space, Magritte called *David's Madame Récamier* (1950) and *Manet's Balcony* (1950) "Perspectives." Obviously, in the short term, the coffin is the only perspective open to the persons David and Manet had represented as living. To appreciate the copies' black humor, one must recall the originals (hence the titles' reference to the painters); the reader of the painting must imagine what is inside the casket. But the use of the term "perspective" to designate a particular genre of art (a new painting enshrouding an old one) is a way of emphasizing how important the painter considers the syntax of his canvas.

This concern for setting the work up as an echo (by doubling spaces and repeating objects)—with the

_____
12 *Ibid.*, no. 194, p. 636.

Zeno's Arrow (*La Flèche de Zénon*), 1964. Oil on canvas, 54 x 65 cm.
Private collection, Brussels

requisite disparity between what is offered and what
is expected, in order to move one from confidence
to disquiet—is enhanced by the activation of surprising
variants. A work's composition makes three elements
cohere: "The object, the thing attached to it in the
shadow of my consciousness and the light in which this
thing is to appear."[13] To the visible world ("the object")
is added the representation in the picture, in the form
of a second object, of what might be thought of as a kind
of shadow cast by the first one, but so meticulously
depicted, without the slightest hesitation in the drawing
or vagueness in the color, that the one stands for the
other: the objective for the subjective, the real for the
imaginary. But this would end up as mere equivocal
equivalences, incongruous meetings, if the face-to-face
encounter did not take place in a certain light, its role

not being to contrast but to assimilate. The shadows are
generally short, and the ambient light even. The role
assigned to light is of a quasi-spiritual kind; it is not
a material given of the world, but a place where the dark
must shine. The picture suggests that the objects are
interchangeable equivalents; it is not static; it seems
to contain something beyond the objects' common
presence. A new world is in preparation. "This pictorial
experiment, which calls the real world into question,"
Magritte wrote in 1945, "leads me to believe in the
infinity of life's unknown possibilities."[14] He was to push
this observation to the point of paradox: if every element
in the world we experience daily raises a question to the
person we are about our origin and our destination, and
if that question is insoluble even in the light of other
elements, could it be that the present world is the
anticipated answer to some unknown question? That
would require human accomplishments to attain the
"quality Poe attributed to the works of a Divinity, where

13 *Ibid.*, "Ligne de vie II," no. 46, p. 144.
14 *Ibid.*, no. 46, p. 145.

cause and effect are reversible."[15] In referring to Poe and alluding to his prose poem *Eureka, An Essay on the Material and Spiritual Universe* (1848, translated into French by Baudelaire), the decidedly materialistic Magritte considers that virtual reality to be a still-hidden aspect of the world.

According to Poe, perfection is something that nature still lacks: "In short, no position can be attained on the wide surface of the *natural* earth, from which an artistical eye, looking steadily, will not find matter of offence in what is termed the 'composition' of the landscape," Ellison confides to the narrator before taking him into the Domain of Arnheim.[16] Through his work, the artist remedies the defects of the world; he perfects its insufficiency, and the public that assists him is part of this evolution. Magritte's paintings are often laid out like a scene from a play; the spectator, an indiscreet onlooker, considers *The Murderer Threatened* (*L'Assassin menacé*, 1926) as if it were a tableau vivant in the theater and watches a shower of clones through a window in *The Month of the Grape Harvest* (*Le Mois des vendanges*, 1959). The theatrical effect is heightened by the curtains Magritte relished decorating the sides of his paintings with, from *The Window* (*La Fenêtre*, 1925) to *Mona Lisa* (*La Joconde*, 1964). Collectors often used curtains to protect their paintings from light and candle smoke, and painters, vying with Parrhasius, put feigned curtains on either side of the subject in a display of skill. In passing from reality to representation, the curtain changed function from useful to symbolic. Its presence in a painting guarantees that the viewer's attention will be focused on what may be teased out of its seeming hiding place: perhaps decrepitude in a *vanitas* or, in a religious painting, the Old Law swept aside by the New. In Magritte's paintings, however, the curtain parts to reveal something familiar placed in a new setting: iron bursts into flame (the fire giving off a dawnlike glow); a boulder hangs motionless in the air, like *Zeno's Arrow* (*La Flèche de Zénon*, 1963). Brood upon an egg with your eyes and a falcon is born, as in *Clairvoyance* (1936). The act of painting becomes a work of revelation, of a reality

unperceived but implicit in visible reality. *Attempting the Impossible* (*Tentative de l'impossible*, 1928) is a kind of manifesto on the action hoped for from painting: to put the finishing touches on the world. The painted curtain is not placed in front of the spectacle on offer, as it is ordinarily, but halfway upstage, between what we know and what we are discovering.

The painting plays the ordinary (the identifiable) against what it harbors within (unveiled by the presence of a double), the visible (whatever is grouped within the canvas's frame) against its transformation (what could be called its becoming). In the composition diagram

Object A	Object B		
Present work	Suggested world		
Material world of oppositions		Virtual site of harmonies	

the development reads from left to right. What is revealed is a shadow cast by the never fully unveiled right-hand side onto the left-hand side. Its role in reality is that of a "secret player." The artist is serving a future society in our time: "Instead of being astonished at the superfluous existence of another world, it is *our only world*, where coincidences surprise us, that we must not lose sight of."[17] Inversion (of sky and sea), duplication (of a shape by its echo), transposition (of a universe —Poe's, Manet's—into another, which actualizes it with modifications), correlation (which forces the mind to wonder about the aberrations in its logic)—these are devices for making the picture appear to have issued from another time, ahead of what it represents.

The Table of the Gods

In its concern to render volume, Magritte's painting, like the body of *The Giantess*, is sculptural. It could also be characterized as monumental: the paintings stand up to enlargement, as demonstrated by *The Enchanted Domain* (*Le Domaine enchanté*, 1953), the mural decoration at Knokke-le-Zoute. Etymologically, the word "monument" designates "that which serves as a reminder." But these pictures are not marked by past events alone; a good many give the impression of being a contemporary souvenir of a period yet to come.

In *The Legend of the Centuries*, an ordinary but minuscule chair placed on an enormous stone rostrum,

15 *Ibid.*, no. 91, p. 326.
16 Poe, *op. cit.* note 3, p. 1272.
17 Magritte, *op. cit.* note 1, no. 135, p. 467.
18 "If I speak of the gods, 'tis that they cover the water, / With their infinite weight, with their flight immortal, / If I speak of the gods, 'tis that they haunt the ether, / If I speak of the gods, 'tis that they are eternal." Raymond Queneau, *Poésies complètes*, vol. 1 (Paris: Gallimard, Bibliothèque de la Pléiade, 1989), "Les Ziaux, IV," p. 66.

the relationship of fleeting existence to mineral eternity is called to mind by cyclopean blocks, which always appear, in our imagination, to have sprung from another world. In his drawings, Victor Hugo was fond of representing his initial in the shape of a throne. Magritte's picture erects a monument to the work of, and becomes a niggardly homage to, the late author. Our language and conceptions bind us to a system we cannot grasp in its totality. We seek the meaning of what is in what surpasses us. Our words are the debris of a language of stone. In *The Art of Conversation IV* (*L'Art de la conversation IV*, 1950), what constitutes a word in our human speech—RÊVE (dream)—is hemmed in by a lithic alphabet. One may assume there are other words crowding around it, in a language so obscure as to be unintelligible, either because it has been expunged from our memory or because it anticipates a time still to come. In the jumble of languages from different times, one word only is common, and offered to the reader-viewer as an access road from his time —ours—to what is not yet.

The Great Table (*La Grande Table*, 1962) shows a gigantic compote placed before the sea. A pulpit appears colossal on one canvas; on another, it is a candle. Furthermore, they are presented to view in a material that renders them alien to our ordinary experience: the apples in the compote are granite; the candle and its flame are petrified. What is not usual has issued, we are led to believe, from another Creation, where beings subtler and more skilled than us have grown large and strong. They know what a fire of stone is. They see enduringly what to us is transitory: a meteor in the sky, a train rushing at full throttle. Impreciseness is a perception of the spirit too slow to grab hold of what passes. However, art is not reduced to rendering the illusion of the instantaneous, but called to evoke a presentiment and premonition of permanence:

The Legend of the Centuries (*La Légende des siècles*), 1952. Gouache on card, 17.8 x 15 cm. The Menil Collection, Houston. Anonymous gift

Si je parle des dieux, c'est qu'ils couvrent la mer
De leur poids infini, de leur vol immortel,
Si je parle des dieux, c'est qu'ils hantent les airs,
Si je parle des dieux, c'est qu'ils sont perpétuels.[18]

In his writings, Magritte does not seem particularly enthusiastic about the works of Raymond Queneau. But these lines are from a poem entitled "Explication des métaphores" (Explanation of Metaphors), and Magritte's oeuvre itself seems to transport us into a space where things are the terms of a particular syntax, where what is mystery today looms in the twilight of a clear and ordinary world.

The originality of the painter's work lies in its evocation of what is not yet, in offering a souvenir of what is still to come. Exhibiting images from a world that could be ulterior to ours, he awakens us to what might formerly have been, through an inverse illusion. The tables laid for us by unseen gods are like those left us by the Titans. In Plato's *Sophist*, the Stranger compares the architect, who builds a house in the traditional manner, and the painter, who conceives a dwelling that is "a man-made dream for waking eyes."[19] Human dreams are made of coherent images that the divinities allow to pass into us, in the morning, through the Gate of Horn. In that respect, the work of the painter, however surprising it may seem to a man who is awake, is the same as that of the divinities who speak their particular language through us. The artist works not on man's time but on the gods': awake, he invents images known to men only when they sleep. A painting by Magritte is neither aberrant nor incoherent; its logic is simply more pointed than what we are used to: "Mystery is not one of reality's possibilities. Mystery is what is absolutely necessary in order for there to be a reality."[20] Without the future world, the present world would crumble. Our memory is marked by a lost ancestral knowledge, just as our imagination is already familiar with what ought to be. This does not mean the artist is a seer, but that his work is to be considered an act of gestation. The painted work does not double reality; it regularly makes visible what the gods reveal only parsimoniously in dreams.

It provides reality with what it lacks in order to be real. The titles assigned to the works could be taken, independently of the representations that they accompany, for a *Bildungsroman* and a theoretical statement: *Collective Invention* (*L'Invention collective*, 1935) responds to *The Call of the Peaks* (*L'Appel des cimes*, 1943); every *Discovery* (*Découverte*, 1927) presupposes the use of *The Key to the Fields* (*La Clé des champs*, 1936); *The Discovery of Fire* (*La Découverte du feu*, 1934) brings reassurance about *The Beyond* (*L'Au-delà*, 1938). This work done, we are not automatically sheltered from *The Anger of the Gods* (*La Colère des dieux*, 1960).

Magritte placed rivers at the edge of his works and regularly included the raging ocean and the calm sea, but he presents them as if already eternal. De Chirico, on the contrary, slipped out-of-place indications, and fragility, into his severe images—the bruise on a banana, the passing shadow of an unseen object, a tremor in the painted line. In the works of Magritte, the paint is applied evenly, the stroke is clear-cut. Dead leaves are not strewn over the prairies; the short gray shadows are not called upon to lengthen. Whether in the light of day or under the quarter moon, time stands still. The painting restores the eternity of the instant: "If I could portray absolute immobility, or rather make one think of absolute immobility, I would achieve, I believe, a certain perfection, because this absolute immobility would correspond to a cessation of thought—thought, which cannot go beyond a certain limit, which cannot comprehend that the world exists."[21] Escaping from current thought would be not only to accede to a state of wisdom but to put an end to history. Like Hegel.

The system, unattainable, could be diagrammed as follows:

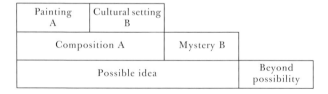

The painting is immersed in a cultural and political environment; this obvious but enigmatic fact points to the existence of a black hole in what we thought was complete. The exchange between A and B is always reciprocal: A is in the process of being fulfilled towards

19 *Sophist*, trans. F.M. Cornford, in *The Complete Dialogues of Plato*, ed. Edith Hamilton and Huntington Cairns (Princeton: Princeton University Press, 1961), p.1014 (266:c).
20 Magritte, *op. cit.* note 1, no.156 (1961), p.525.
21 *Ibid.*, no.187 (Interview with Jean Neyens, 1965), p.604.

B, but B reveals the incompleteness of A, without absolute immobility ever being attained. Normally, the name of God is assigned to a state of dreamed-of stability, in a present world.

The painting and its title in turn become a question and answer. "To be able to answer the question 'What is the *meaning* of these images?' would correspond to making Meaning, the Impossible, resemble a possible idea." Magritte thus reiterated in like terms a remark made a short time earlier: "Meaning is the Impossible for possible thought."[22] Which means what? Painting does not state ideas, does not express feelings, does not specify sensations; it offers a vision of what is becoming and therefore eludes our discourse. Painting shows an impossible that is compatible with our possible world. Its true space is the dark area of thought that engulfs Lichtenberg's knife, which lost its blade and never had a handle. What resists our understanding lends a radiance to what we think we see: "It is mystery that enlightens knowledge."[23] The absence of an immediately formulatable Meaning gives the Impossible its chance to become probable. The painting of Magritte is that of a man whose memory is filled with recollections of the gods to come.

*

There is nothing secret behind a curtain; the essential takes place on both sides of the space it divides, of what is and of what is to be caused to be. Magritte does not present a remarkable scene, such as a battle of Alexander or one of Venus's sensual adventures, but a place where it is possible to suggest the presence, in what is, of what cannot be seen. Painting is an exercise in suggesting what reality lacks in order to become itself. Curiously, a painting or a piece of writing draws its strength of being from what is missing from reality, from what it suggests the nonexistence of in that which exists. Artistic activity seeks to put the finishing touches on the world, to make visible in it what it aspires to be. In a picture, the appropriate thing is not to make nature a fair captive, but a fine illusion. Painting is not vain, but a precursor: by means of what is at present an artifice, it makes what is to come appear.

The viewer is not called upon to derive enjoyment from what he sees, but to be disturbed by what escapes him.

22 *Ibid.*, no. 108 (1954), p. 376, and no. 105, p. 363.
23 *Ibid.*, no. 118 (1955), p. 418.

Magritte. Photograph by Roland d'Ursel

Patrick Roegiers

The Self-Resistant René Magritte

Unlike many painters, including Bonnard, Khnopff and Bacon, René Magritte enjoyed taking photographs and made no secret of it. He took pictures both for personal purposes and entertainment, to amuse himself and his friends by setting up and portraying imaginary scenes of pure invention, in much the same way as he did with home movies. In a more traditional, strictly pictorial register, he also used photography to record models, props and poses as an aid to reproducing them on canvas. Each of these three distinct, independent and wholly complementary categories of his photography is worth considering in its own right. They form an entryway into the private life of a man who was deeply linked to the expression of his art, while also providing an escape from it, to visualize fantasies and amusing skits that serve to transport us laughing and sniggering behind the scenes of his painting.

Documents of the Ordinary

Like anyone else, René Magritte took photographs as souvenirs of his travels and holidays. We see him bare chested, on a bicycle, at Knokke in 1933-4 with Paul Nougé and Georgette; in sandals and short sleeves, on the dike with Paul Colinet; on horseback and, like any Belgian on summer holiday, pedaling a *cuistax*. An average man in average circumstances, without great financial means—he did not become rich until age sixty—Magritte appears as he really is in his everyday middle-class life, someone who eats at regular hours, paints in a Sunday suit (which is not so usual), lives in an ordinary home, has friends over, invites them to dinner, shows them his latest work, chatters, answers his abundant correspondence and is a fairly avid reader. By his own admission leading a drab existence, Magritte documented his own reality, but also that of the everyday, which is at once extraordinary and banal, eccentric and organized, delirious and well-regulated: he looks after his budgerigars; he walks his dog—one of a series of Pomeranians, usually answering to the same name, which he took everywhere he went and doted on to the point of having one of them stuffed. Early to bed,

rather indifferent towards others, more intelligent than cultivated, stubborn, industrious, rarely short of ideas —even though he copied, indeed parodied, himself copiously—he was capable of doing a painting per day while he was "perpetually flat broke," until 1945, when his work finally began to sell.

Tirelessly questioning, dourly domineering, a thin-skinned homebody, if he was cunningly calculating and openly scatological at times, Magritte, a Surrealist at heart, was more given to taciturn melancholy than is generally thought. Of course, he read Baudelaire and Pound and listened to Georgette play Satie, but he smoked constantly (dark tobacco) and in photos used a cigarette as a crutch, to project an impression of composure. He stopped doing this once he assumed the role of Magritte, but not yet having done so, he appeared as he was: robust, thickset and square, disinclined to sports and exercise, not particularly attractive or charming—not to mention his accent, with its heavily rrrrolled r's—gray eyes in an oval face like a Chinese vase, thick brown hair, a gruff fellow from the Borinage, and paunchy, once he was no longer the young man in a tailored suit with fitted waist who posed with Georgette on his knees, caressed her tenderly on the cheek on 28 June 1922, the day they were married in Saint-Josse-ten-Noode. In fact, photography records Georgette's daily life, in his painting and in his life. It is through photos that he made known his love for her, affectionately framing her in a bathing suit and imitation pearl necklace, stretched out on the sand, wearing a white dress, open-armed in front of a barge, embracing herself, seen from behind, her hands placed alongside her bust, and even with thighs bared in a delightful erotic pose, when he incited her to raise her skirt in the Ardennes, in 1947, with his white Pomeranian looking on.

Georgette, pictured smoking with a view to an advertising project for Boule Nationale cigarettes in 1934, was his muse, his unerring guide, the woman who stood behind him, his accomplice and only painting model, beside whom he posed in 1929, his brow surmounted by a hair-raising frizzy mop, evidence that he, who had not yet become the apostle of the ironico-Belgian tradition, followed the fads and took a long time to find himself. While awaiting success, he went about in shirt sleeves on the arm of his better half, their little Pom at their side, in Josaphat Park in Schaerbeek, or on the dike at Knokke-le-Zoute, a stone's throw from the Casino. In all these pictures, Magritte looks thoroughly natural, without distinguishing features, desperately banal, which perhaps at bottom he was. This is also the case when he poses in a straw hat in 1928 at Le Perreux-sur-Marne; or in a regular fedora and coat, sitting on a bench, his hands on his knees, beside Georgette and Agui Ubac; or wearing a conventional hat before boarding a Sabena flight bound for New York; or finally with a Stetson on his head during a trip to Texas for his 1965 retrospective in Houston. And he looks just as ordinary in some group photos, like the one Albert Van Loock took on the doorstep of the bar La Fleur en papier doré in Brussels, in which, for once, the clan chief blends into the circle, and even in the well-known snapshot with Marcel Duchamp, Max Ernst and Man Ray in Amsterdam, in October 1966, during the Bill Copley exhibition, where Magritte smiles shyly, dressed in a dark raincoat, glasses propped above his forehead.

However, for Magritte, every image, no matter how dull, had a meaning. Using the still image as a direct means of approaching the visible, by 1928 he was toying with the Photomat at the Jardin des Plantes—as was Max Ernst at the same time and, later, Paul Nougé—trying out one of the first instant photo booths in Paris (the earliest had appeared in New York in 1926). He is pictured with his eyes closed, as in Man Ray's *Surrealist Checkerboard* (1934), sixteen small photos showing all the members of the Surrealist group with their eyes closed, a rebus on vision, on the enigma of sight, arranged as a border around *Je ne vois pas la [femme] cachée dans la forêt* (*I Do Not See the [Woman] Hidden in the Forest*). Similar photomontages were conceived by E. L. T. Mesens and Salvador Dalí, who issued *Le Phénomène de l'extase* (*The Phenomenon of Ecstasy*, 1933) in the form of a puzzle. For Magritte, who was interested in the medium's specific possibilities, photography partook above all of mystery. It is that melancholy art, with a proclivity to the funereal as portrayed by solitary beings dressed like undertakers' assistants, wearing a lab coat and a plain hat, holding vigil in an impossible mourning that can easily enough be attributed to the irreparable loss of his mother, who drowned herself in the Sambre and was fished out, her white nightgown matted to her face, clinging like a shroud to her lifeless body. Once he had achieved fame, Magritte posed so much as himself, like a character who had stepped out of one of his paintings, that, with hindsight, it looks odd to see him photographed the way he was, in a raincoat or bathing suit on the dike or at the beach, with Georgette and Jackie, the black or white Pomeranian. But also from behind in a vacant lot, where he was not strolling by chance, and between two doors in a web of corridors, in front of the penetrating and restless lens of Roland d'Ursel. In these apparently anodyne compositions, the placement of the figure in space, the relationship to the decor and accessories, the range of the light and sky, the weight of the architecture, in short, the heft of reality—everything evokes and leads back to his paintings, which he seems less to have stepped out of than to be attempting to enter, turning his back in his ratine coat and black hat.

The Invisible Adventure

Magritte was an avid movie fan—cowboys and Indians, gangsters, comedies—and at home with his group of friends he watched rented films by Sinoel and other diverting, unpretentious comedies like *Coup dur chez les mous* and *Madame et son auto*, which he preferred to *Les 400 coups* of François Truffaut, whom he disliked. Influenced by the silent movies of Mack Sennett, king of slapstick, and crime movies like Louis Feuillade's *Fantômas*—an object of the Surrealists' enthusiasm that surely inspired the emblematic painting *The Murderer Threatened* (*L'Assassin menacé*, 1927)—in 1956, he bought an 8 mm home movie camera and, giving free reign to his sense of the unaccustomed and his taste for jokes and disguises, created a series of short films with his friends and their wives, whom he cast in absurd, strange and hilarious skits and directed like a severe taskmaster, as conscientious as he was farcical and fun-loving. All together they formed a mischievous troupe, a community of jokesters—oh, those incorrigible *zwanzeurs*!—who disguised themselves, were wonderstruck, simulating, overacting, having a ball, each stepping out of their, sometimes contritely, accepted bourgeois role to become actors for the duration of a take or a shot. Attesting to how "very tiresome" professional cinema was in his opinion, Magritte indulged in unusual and unheard-of discoveries, thought up from shreds of scenario, entirely improvised and visibly interpreted. For it was essential that everything be *acted*, which was heightened by a farcical use of the mask that links Magritte to Ensor's grand Belgian tradition of disguise, but also quotes and refers to his painting, like the movie still from *Le Loup rouge* (*The Red Wolf*) of two figures veiled in towels, a striking evocation of his famous canvas *The Lovers* (*Les Amants*, 1928).

Magritte reinforced his vocation of anti-painter by distracting himself from his "deep-rooted pessimism" in brief clownish escapades that exude a familial, good-natured, meek and cheerful Surrealism, but more subversive than it appears here, judging from the salvaged bits of film butchered by unscrupulous scissors. These short films, orchestrated as if they were paintings, with a duly established cast, conceived from brief scenarios to a specified length, with props and ideas to develop, and with the participants even being asked to "show some genius", found a direct continuation in the photos taken between 1928 and 1955, during his leisure, with the same henchmen as bit players, whose indecorous portraits he took in situations concocted to convey a frame of mind. Yet another spin-off are those pictures taken in private, supposedly the most common, places, which he used in order to free himself from an alienated reality, drawing forth from the most tedious banality the strange, invisible and disturbing, as well as the inexplicable and unthinkable, dreams, menace and madness. Through these scenes that fall within "the systematic search for an upsetting effect," Magritte, the white-collar worker of the easel and creator of enigmas, intentionally carried on anti-artistic activity, working not as a model employee or as an erudite aesthete, but as a mischievous prankster. To see in another way, to show what the eye does not see, to create an "other world," to get out of the rut of the familiar, to invent enigmas, to address not questions without answers but questions that are not asked, that had not yet been asked other than by the painter himself (as he said, "psychology concerns itself with false mysteries")—that is the object of these *stupefying* images. The fruit of a well thought-out spontaneity, all these conform to the principle of ironic distance and bring off the tour de force of combining photography at its most instantaneous with picture-taking as a device of playful, subtly elaborated representation.

The realization of these images, which are never symbolic, brought the nonconformist painter back to the Belgian coast, to Knokke and Coxyde, the

Ardennes, Soignes Forest, to Antwerp, Brussels, Beersel, Le Perreux, Versailles, Sénart Forest, where his friends posed with their heads between their legs in *The Natural Graces* (*Les Grâces naturelles*, 1929), climbed into an old jalopy, scaled iron gates in *The Descent of La Courtille* (*La Descente de La Courtille,* 1928), or mimed a silly greeting. It brought him as well to Lessines, which he detested so much that he referred to trips to his native town as "expeditions," though in 1935 he took some of his best photos there, like *The Star of Stone* (*L'Etoile de pierre*), *The Apparition* (*L'Apparition*), *The Pharaohs* (*Les Pharaons*), *The Bonheur du Jour* (*Le Bonheur du Jour*) and *The Labor of Hercules* (*Le Travail d'Hercule*). To do what one must not do, to commit acts that are forbidden or considered unseemly, is the crucial engagement of these weird and zany scenes, which were later bestowed by Louis Scutenaire (who posed asleep on the train tracks in *The Fine Journey* [*Le Beau Voyage*], 1937) with titles akin to those of the paintings and grouped together as *La Fidélité des images* (The Faithful Images) and in another album soberly entitled *Photographies de Magritte*.[1] "To think an image means to *see* an image," Magritte confided apropos of these optical experiments, where the unexpected originates from ordinary attitudes and situations as well as from everyday objects diverted from their function and turned into props—all extremely simple and banal, insignificant and with no import beyond that normally allotted to them, except that they must "eloquently reveal their existence." And without exalting their inherent poetry, as was common currency with Surrealism, but on the contrary treating them as prosaically as possible. These disturbing and droll photographs are all very logical, without fictional

The Stone Guests (*Le Festin de pierre*). Photograph. Paul and René Magritte, Marcel Mariën, Brussels, 1942

1 *La Fidélité des images. René Magritte, le cinématographe et la photographie* (Brussels: Lebeer-Hossmann, 1976); *Photographies de Magritte* (Paris: Contrejour, 1982).

41

The Eminence Grise (L'Eminence grise). Photograph.
René Magritte, Belgian coast, 1938

excesses or emphatic demonstrations of the imagination. Magritte excelled at suffusing humble objects with an astonishing aura—bricks, shoes and fireplaces take on a novel dimension if you eat them, hide your face behind them, or use them like a comfortable bedspring.

Realizing the importance and the recurrence of simple objects in his oeuvre—wolves, tubas, hats, candles, masks, paintings and books, as well as balusters, sleigh bells, birds, apples, curtains, glasses and loaves of bread—we cannot help being struck by the use and unusual meaning of domestic utensils and bric-à-brac. The same is true of the brick pile, the base of an imaginary pyramid at a construction site in Lessines, at the foot of which Magritte carries on like an intrepid explorer, and the bricks he eats, sinking his teeth into them with gusto, in the company of his brother Paul and Marcel Mariën in *The Stone Guests* (*Le Festin de pierres*, 1942), thus carrying the notion of the feast to its literal and logical conclusion. Or think of that curious view taken on the Belgian coast in 1938, where he poses in a black bathing suit with shoulder straps, an open book hung on his back, offering a Surrealist vision completely staggering in the simplicity of its governing idea. All the more so because, in a snapshot

taken just afterwards on the same occasion, showing him from the front—potbellied, his arms at his sides, the top of his bathing suit lowered—the spell has been broken. This about-face reveals how poetry is created from nothing and how reality reclaims its rights the minute you turn your back on it.

This photograph, entitled *The Eminence Grise*, is worth pausing over. Magritte is forty. In a dark bathing suit, facing away from the camera, he turns towards the horizon, from which the outstretched beach, cut off by an arm of the sea, separates him. This scene, as much a portrait as a self-portrait, ensues from the painter's stance vis-à-vis reality. Magritte did not like posing any more than he liked painting portraits. By showing his back to the camera, he expresses a refusal of his presence and sidesteps the conventional codes of photography, whereby a person's back is not supposed to occupy the foreground. On the other hand, this attitude, though negative at first glance, accentuates the singularity of the open book hung on his back. For, while Magritte contemplates the beach, we stare at the book, bearer of marks, characters and expressions, which thus becomes the "cover" of the bathing suit. By glorifying the object's presence, Magritte has made it the figurative vehicle of his thoughts; by exhibiting the book in counterpoint to his averted head, it becomes the equivalent of the model's face, allowing his thoughts to be read more easily than his face would. But there is a third element in this snapshot where the painter conveys "in covert terms" his familiar obsession with the double face. Although at first glance it may appear that Magritte is staring out at the deserted beach, on closer inspection, one realizes he is looking at his shadow, which accounts for his position relative to the sun. For Magritte, a shadow is light's most palpable means of becoming visible. In staring at his shadow, the model raises the issue of what he designates as his visual appearance. Magritte shows himself to be true to his principles in this self-portrait once removed. In mocking his image, he confronts the visible and suggests, off the cuff, the existence of what seems invisible but, to his eye, is actually something visible hidden by the visible.

In intrinsically photographic settings, admirably simple once you have come up with the idea, Magritte enjoyed bringing out the incongruous and unwonted in the most ordinary situations to focus the beholder's attention on the vague presence of mystery. So it is, too, with the disconcerting gesture of hiding one's face —which generally takes pride of place in a photo—with sandals, as Louis Scutenaire and Paul Nougé do in *The Plantigrades* (*Les Plantigrades*, 1935), and Nougé again in *The Giant* (*Le Géant*, 1937), brandishing a checkerboard in front of his face, heralding the apples that appear before so many bowler-hatted heads in the paintings. Incidentally, images by Nougé, as well as by Georges Thiry, are often attributed to Magritte. Nougé produced an experimental series exploring absence and emptiness, decoy and representation, the play of truth and the illusion of likelihood, the wakefulness of a dream and the sleep of reason, in an astonishing series of nineteen photographs taken during the winter of 1929–30 and later published by Marcel Mariën as *Subversion des images* (Subversive Images).[2] These are fascinating and very elaborate surreal visions, where Magritte himself figures among *The Drinkers* (*Les Buveurs*), clinking invisible glasses (telepathic communication), and in the dumbstruck group in front of a fireplace in *The Birth of the Object* (*La Naissance de l'objet*). Nougé, whom Magritte met in 1925 and who remained his accomplice until their final rupture in September 1952, imagined paradoxical affirmations and embryonic instances of "upsetting disorientation" in his quest to flush out the frightening at the core of the familiar, the unspeakable in the ordinary, in short, for a visual and mental way of interrogating the world, in the image of *The Woman Frightened by a Piece of String* (*La Femme effrayée par une ficelle*) and *The Cut Eyelashes* (*Les Cils coupés*), an ironic reference to Luis Buñuel's and Salvador Dalí's *Un Chien andalou* (*An Andalusian Dog*, 1928).

"I believe there is only one thing that still can amaze me, and that is to live," Magritte writes in his lucid letter of rupture to Nougé, with whom he shared, despite their divergent views, the art of hijacking the habits and codes of the bourgeois society he was answerable to, donning the upstanding citizen's conformist uniformity of dress, assuming his framework of life, rigid attitudes and civility. Still, Magritte remained an iconoclast, given to a systematic mockery, partial to Schopenhauer's nihilism, adept at delivering a kick up the ass with an almost Dadaistic gusto, as reported by Scutenaire, with whom he became acquainted in 1926. Conceived as individual images, devoid of serial narration, anchored in space, Magritte's photographs, meant to resist all explanation, are never generated by automatism but, on the contrary, always result from a process of creation that is well

2 Paul Nougé, *Subversion des images* (Brussels: Les lèvres nues, 1968).

thought out, planned, studied, discussed among friends. Thus, they have nothing to do with the formally Surrealist photographs of Marcel Lefrancq and Raoul Ubac, based on experimentation with the plastic possibilities of the medium (singeing, solarization, double exposure and superimposition). Instead, Magritte relied on the tangible reality of objects, situations and decors as a means of reaching the darkest zones of the imagination, and regarded photography as an amateur undertaking as well as a field for experimentation and amusement fueled by a penchant for ransacking, subversion and an all-powerful irony.

In this sense, one may say that a lightness, an alacrity, a freedom of invention stand out in his photographs, on a level equaling the two phases of stylistic rupture in his painting: the "Sunlit," or "Renoir," period (1943–7), a pastiche of Impressionism; and the "Vache" period (1947–8), which jeered at Fauvism and was given a disastrous reception in Paris. Both periods were conceived in a great elation of form and thought, in bright, shrill tones, of an undeniable modernity,

The Giant (*Le Géant*). Photograph. Paul Nougé, Belgian coast, 1937

Love (*L'Amour*). Photograph. Georgette and
René Magritte, Le Perreux-sur-Marne, 1928

Magritte painting *Attempting the Impossible* (*Tentative de
l'impossible*). Photograph. Le Perreux-sur-Marne, 1928

for the supreme purpose of *displeasing*. As if he knew
in advance how pleasing his painting would be if true
to what was expected of it, later re-conjugating
it repeatedly, ad nauseam, to the point of self-parody,
Magritte, the seditious inventor, anticlerical and
antimilitary, a brazen blasphemer who was exasperated
by common sense and plain reason, endeavoring to
"do what must not be done in painting," loosed the reins
to his nonconformity and produced pure anti-painting,
stimulating and so fresh that it stands thirty-five years
after his death as the most fertile and impertinent of all
his oeuvre.

Attempting the Impossible

Contrary to the widespread notion, Magritte's use
of photography as an aid in creating his paintings was
not infrequent. In fact, he first did so as early as 1928,
with *Love* (*L'Amour*), where the painter, in white shirt
and tie, wearing the plaid carpet slippers that would

resurface in the "Vache" period, labors palette in hand
to paint his better half, who poses barefoot in a bathing
suit. The masterstroke of the resulting painting,
Attempting the Impossible (*Tentative de l'impossible*), was
to depict her incomplete, still in the process of creation,
with a patch of nude body left unpainted, while he,
wearing a three-piece suit, works away with the tip
of his brush on her left shoulder. No doubt taken
in the apartment in Le Perreux-sur-Marne, at 101
Avenue de Rosny, this photodocument (of which
there is a variant on the opposite axis, with the painter,
in a double-breasted suit, at the foot of the work
in progress) indicates that Magritte at times painted
from photos. He did so partly to spare Georgette, his
only model, from lengthy posing sessions, but also
in order to reproduce as closely as possible his carefully
gestated idea. This touching staged photo—and who
took it?—shows that Magritte practiced photography
as play, painting as work and art as a profession.

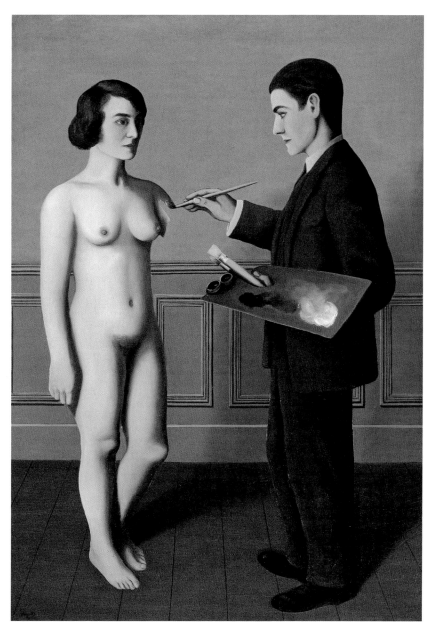

Attempting the Impossible (*Tentative de l'impossible*),
1928. Oil on canvas, 116 x 81 cm.
Toyota Municipal Museum of Art, Toyota Aichi

This simple, effective and perfectly studied device is found in many studies where Georgette, radiant, docile and confident, the source of his almost inexhaustible inspiration, lent herself without balking, to judge by her expression, to the many situations her husband put her in, such as posing in profile holding a leaf and a glass of water in 1944 for *The Rights of Man* (*Les Droits de l'homme*). And the same goes for his closest friends: Scutenaire posed in a plaid suit, his pants tucked into his tall socks pulled up like knickers, a squeegee on his back in place of a rifle, for *Universal Gravitation* (*La Gravitation universelle*, 1943), as well as for *God on the Eighth Day* (*Dieu, le huitième jour*, 1937). Taken in the garden at Rue Esseghem in Jette, where the Magrittes settled upon their return from Paris, this photograph served as a preliminary study

for *The Healer* (*Le Thérapeute*, 1941), of which there are at least four versions, one of them a sculpture.

Magritte himself posed as well, palette in hand, painting *Clairvoyance* (1936), where he depicts himself sketching a bird while eyeing an egg; the photo, which includes both the canvas in progress and an image representing it, sets the painted self-portrait up as a "picture in the picture." Similarly, he may be recognized as *The Spy* (*L'Espion*, 1927), peering through a keyhole, plainly a parallel to the voyeuristic posture of a photographer with his eye glued to the viewfinder. And again, he lent his features to *The Magician* (*Le Sorcier*, 1951), executed in lieu of a portrait of Alexander Iolas, who delayed too long in sending the prints Magritte had requested in a letter of 16 May 1951, charging the

Universal Gravitation (*La Gravitation universelle*), 1943.
Oil on canvas, 100 x 73 cm.
Private collection

The Destroyer (*Le Destructeur*).
Photograph. Louis Scutenaire,
Brussels, 1943

Paul Nougé, *The Birth of the Object* (*La Naissance de l'objet*). Photograph, 1929

The Spy (*L'Espion*), 1928. Oil on canvas, 54 x 73 cm. Private collection

capricious dealer with the conditions of their execution: "I must have *fairly quickly* three photos of you, taken by one of your friends with an easily obtainable, ordinary camera. I am enclosing instructions about how to proceed."[3] Tired of being left hanging, Magritte painted himself frontally and easily identifiable in a three-piece suit, eating with four hands. "Neither those obsessed with movement nor those obsessed with immobility will find this image to their taste," he warned.

It is a patent fact that Magritte did not like to do portraits. The most glaring proof is provided by that of Edward James whom Magritte met in Paris through Dalí. James, a great collector, poet and writer, was close to the Surrealists (among them Man Ray, who did his portrait in 1937), a friend of Duchamp and Picasso, and sponsor of the magazine *Minotaure* from 1933 to 1939. Invited to decorate his house at 35 Wimpole Street in 1937, Magritte spent five weeks in London where, during a lecture at the London Gallery founded by Mesens, he expounded upon his creative process. And he painted three canvases at the request of his host: *On the Threshold of Freedom* (*Au seuil de la liberté*), *The Red Model* (*Le Modèle rouge*) and *Youth Illustrated* (*La Jeunesse illustrée*), as vouched for by photos of the artist at work in a white apron, from the back, seated and standing. Man Ray's portrait of the fabulously wealthy banker served

as the model for the painting *The Pleasure Principle, Portrait of Edward James* (*Le Principe de plaisir ...*, 1937), where the sitter's head is replaced by a dazzling gleam of light. The blinding *flash* makes James a man with invisible facial features or worse, faceless, as first appears in an ink sketch entitled *Failed Portrait* (*Portrait manqué*), conceived the year before, evidence that all Magritte had to do was develop his idea so long as he had found it. In a second canvas, entitled *Not to Be Reproduced* (*La Reproduction interdite*), he painted James from behind, standing in front of a mirror, with the French edition of Poe's *Narrative of Arthur Gordon Pym* at his side on the ledge of the fireplace. Incidentally, on a rainy Sunday afternoon in December 1965, Magritte went to the Bronx to see the house of the poet he so admired. In this split portrait, it is not the model's face that is reflected in the mirror as it would be in reality, but the back of his head, the reverse of the image ensnared in its representation. Thus, with as much art as irony, Magritte transforms the chore of the commissioned portrait, which is usually a faithful copy of the subject's character, into a formally photographic meditation on the false truth of appearances and the illusory reproduction of the mirror, snare of reflections, the essential medium of photography.

The Impossible Portrait

Through the prism of photography, René Magritte drew an intangible and no doubt impossible portrait

3 David Sylvester, ed., *René Magritte. Catalogue raisonné*, vol. 3 (Houston: Menil Foundation/Antwerp: Fonds Mercator, 1993), p.186.

of himself. Whether he posed with a tuba on his head
for Suzi Gablik; disguised as Fantômas in *The Barbarian*
(*Le Barbare*, 1928; a parody he revisited in *The Flame
Rekindled* [*Retour de flamme*], 1943); wearing a hat and
a dark overcoat in front of the red brick wall of his house
which appears in so many of his canvases; feigning sleep
or reading like one of his characters; or donning
a disguise that conceals imposture and denotes
anonymity, like the bowler hat, which was just as much
an emblem of respectability as it was a clown's attribute
in film comedies of the 1930s—Magritte was never
anyone but himself, played only at being himself.
Denouncing the impersonality of uniform models,
he is at once himself and the neutral figure of his
interchangeable and anonymous characters, all dressed
the same and wearing a bowler hat, as did his father
—who for a time worked as a tailor, while his mother
was a milliner—assuming the impassive air of a traveling
salesman or a clerk in their Sunday best. He who in his
painting was so nonconformist, malcontent, subversive
and insubordinate, plundering his own work at certain
quickly stifled periods, persistently strove to take
on the appearance of a quiet fellow. Transparent
in its simplicity yet impenetrable, assuring him
of the continued maintenance of his role, the uniform
he adopted as he grew more famous enabled him
to disappear under a disguise and say with a laugh,
"You will never know who I am."

For *The Enchanted Domain* (*Le Domaine enchanté*, 1953),
the large mural executed at the Knokke Casino in six
months by assistants under his supervision, in which
he reused various themes from his paintings, he provided
an indication of scale by climbing the ladder set
up in front of it. He posed for Bill Brandt in front
of a portrait of Georgette in 1965, wearing a hat and suit,
candle in hand, in a detective novel atmosphere, pleased
so to salute his status as painter of nocturnal light and
master of mystery. He posed beside one of his paintings
on the easel; or hiding his face behind an effigy
of Georgette; or holding *The Eternally Obvious* (*L'Evidence
éternelle*, 1949), which shows his wife's body in separate
pieces. When he appears in a summer suit,
or houndstooth check, wearing glasses, his hair neatly
combed, handkerchief tucked in his pocket, once he has
achieved world fame, one realizes how ordinary he looks,
how insignificant, woefully average, the minute he stops
playing the role of painter. That is the case when
he poses without his attributes for Roland d'Ursel,
in Rue Esseghem, cigarette in hand, or with a Mexican

God on the Eighth Day (*Dieu, le huitième jour*). Photograph.
René Magritte, Rue Esseghem, Brussels, 1937

The Healer (*Le Thérapeute*), 1962. Gouache on paper,
35.5 x 27.5 cm. Private collection

straw hat, only to wince the next instant, wiping the floor with the venerable posture of the official artist in the twinkling of an eye.

Often sullen, Magritte chose his words carefully, even if he intentionally made mistakes with the names of people he didn't know. Long disdained in Paris, which he called *Piras* in a letter to Irène Hamoir (6 April 1948), Magritte took the tram or bus to go into town, playing chess at the Cirio Café, next to the Stock Exchange —less brilliantly than Duchamp, whom he welcomed to Brussels and placed in good hands. Much as he admired Xavier Mellery, Fernand Khnopff and William Degouve de Nuncques, and spent his time secluded with Georgette in the living room of his house that must definitely be considered the common place of his childless petit bourgeois existence as a sedate and unexciting fellow, Magritte was a phlegmatic thinker, a "decalcomaniac" of desire, with a caustic wit, coolly delirious, methodical in his mode of creation. He was also a logician of the imagination, a bon vivant, licentious and cocky, who sealed insidiously academic mystifications beneath a false air of the inveterate plagiarist. Surrealism is a manner of being, and no one could have embodied it for Belgium better than Magritte. The artist who waited until the age of sixty for recognition, who boasted that he never spoiled a painting—but had so much trouble selling them at the start (the first having been bought in 1924 for 100 Belgian francs, the denomination of the banknote duly pilloried by Marcel Mariën and Léo Dohmen in a photocollage lampoon from 1962 entitled *Grande Baisse [Great Bargain Sale]*)—played the appearance of appearances to the hilt. Through the disguise that constituted him and identified him with his work, sometimes to the point of caricaturing it, he attested a feigned subjection to reality and played, as a good dialectician, upon the art of resemblances and of multiplying and nesting them: the self and the other, or the other himself, but also the image of the person and the image of the image, becoming therefore the image in person and, in the end, the figurative person or the imaged figure, thus lending credence to Valéry's sound creed: "That which resembles nothing does not exist."

Towards the end of his life, Magritte opened his bourgeois interior to the American photographer Duane Michals,[4] who made much more than a photo essay on a painter he admired. By means of superimpression, Michals allowed him to be his own double, just as Magritte himself had given a double face to Georgette in a floral print summer dress, vest and white socks on the beach in 1939, in scarcely differing poses based on double figures from his paintings. But Magritte also indulged in various pranks, appearing, disappearing and multiplying, sleeping on the sofa in the living room, awash in the dreamed arcana of his world, doffing his hat to posterity, poking fun at his glory, in his charming cottage at 97 Rue des Mimosas, and making it clearly understood that if he has assumed the appearance of a "salon painter," he is definitely not a Sunday painter. No longer playing at being, but accepting at last to appear for real, comfortably ensconced in his shoes, his face tired-looking, his features drawn, his potbelly protruding, he poses in a striped double-breasted suit, fists in his pockets, before the admirable lens of Georges Thiry, at Schaerbeek, in 1959. And then, one last time, the year before he died of pancreatic cancer at the age of sixty-nine, on August 15, 1967. In haste to be done with it, he replied, somewhat unsociably, when that other great but still too little known photographer asked: "I beg your pardon, master, may I take your picture?" "Yes, but hurry up."[5]

Magritte in Schaerbeek, 1959. Photograph by Georges Thiry

4 Duane Michals, *A Visit with Magritte* (Matrix, 1981).
5 *Georges Thiry, la photographie …* (Liège: Yellow Now/Charleroi: Musée de la Photographie, 2002).

Magritte: The Use of Painting

∧ *A Box at the Theater* (*La Loge* or *L'Etrangère*), 1925. Oil on canvas, 63 x 82 cm.
Private collection

> *The Magician's Accomplices* (*Les Complices du magicien*), 1926. Oil on canvas, 139 x 105 cm.
Private collection

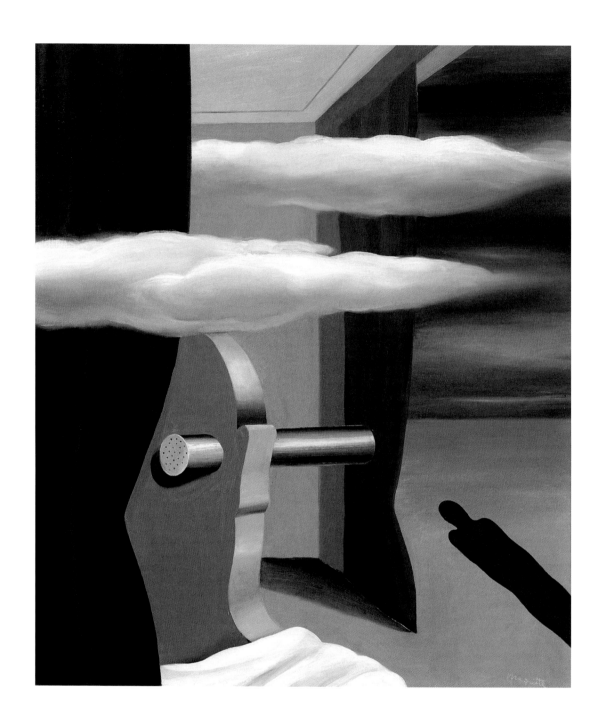

∧ *Sensational News* (*La Grande Nouvelle*), 1926. Oil on canvas, 62 x 81 cm.
  Private collection, Belgium

< *The Desert Catapult* (*La Catapulte du désert*), 1926. Oil on canvas, 75 x 65 cm.
  Private collection, Belgium

∧ *The Silvered Chasm* (*Le Gouffre argenté*), 1926. Oil on canvas, 75 x 65 cm.
   The Berardo Collection – Sintra Museum of Modern Art, Lisbon

< *The Birth of the Idol* (*La Naissance de l'idole*), 1926. Oil on canvas, 120 x 80 cm.
   Private collection

∧ *The Threshold of the Forest* (*Le Seuil de la forêt*), 1926. Oil on canvas, 75 x 65 cm.
   Collection Konrad Klapheck, Düsseldorf

> *The Secret Double* (*Le Double Secret*), 1927. Oil on canvas, 114 x 162 cm.
   Centre Georges Pompidou, Paris, Musée national d'Art moderne /
   Centre de Création industrielle

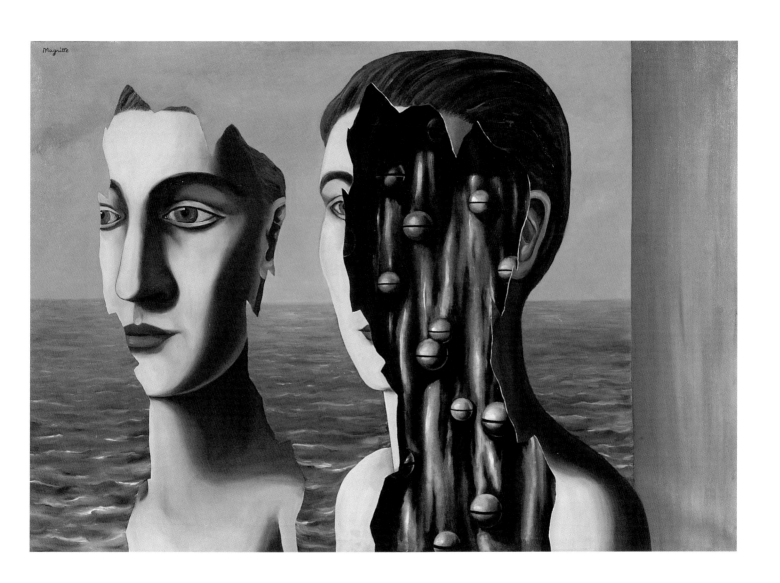

60

∧ *An End to Contemplation* (*La Fin des contemplations*), 1927. Oil on canvas, 73 x 100 cm.
   The Menil Collection, Houston

< *Polar Light* (*La Lumière du pôle*), 1926 or 1927. Oil on wood, 139 x 105 cm.
   Private collection, courtesy de Pury & Luxembourg, Zurich

The Murderous Sky (*Le Ciel meurtrier*), 1927. Oil on canvas, 73 x 100 cm.
Centre Georges Pompidou, Paris, Musée national d'Art moderne/
Centre de Création industrielle

∧ *The Scent of the Abyss* (*Le Parfum de l'abîme*), 1928. Oil on canvas, 54 x 73 cm.
Private collection

> *Atlantis* (*L'Atlantide*), 1927. Oil on canvas, 100 x 72.4 cm.
Rose Art Museum, Brandeis University, Waltham, Massachusetts.
Gift of Mr. and Mrs. Eric Estorick, London

The Secret Player (*Le Joueur secret*), 1927. Oil on canvas, 152 x 195 cm.
Musées Royaux des Beaux-Arts de Belgique, Brussels, inv. 11631

The Murderer Threatened (L'Assassin menacé), 1926. Oil on canvas, 150.4 x 195.2 cm.
The Museum of Modern Art, New York. Kay Sage Tanguy Fund, 1966

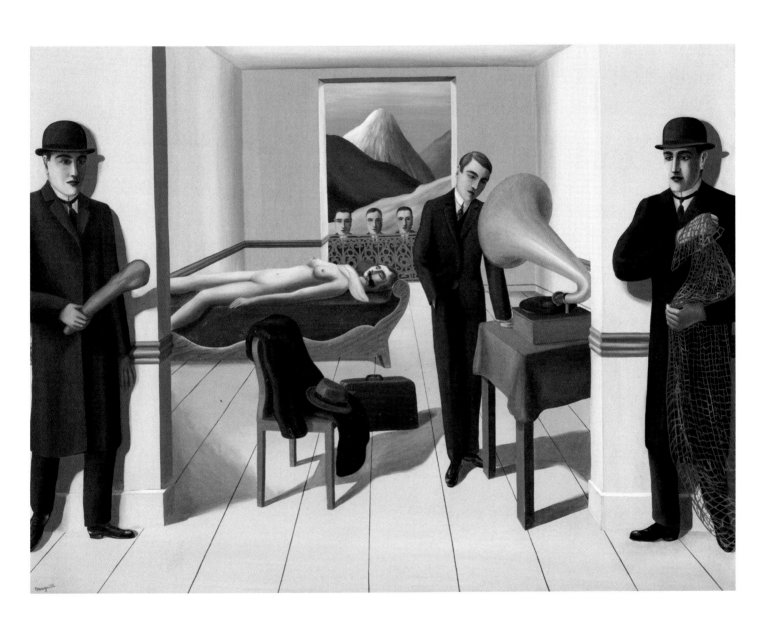

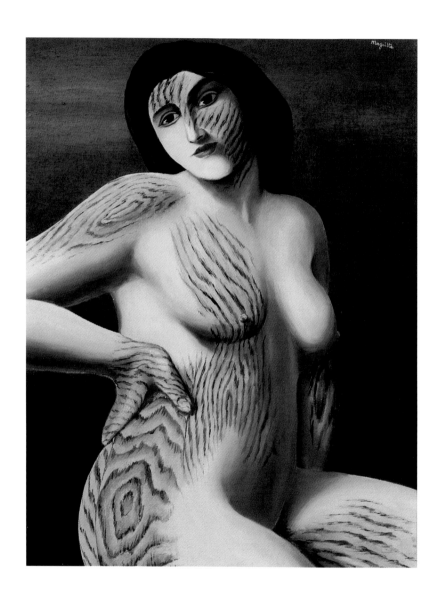

∧ *Discovery* (*Découverte*), 1927. Oil on canvas, 65 x 50 cm.
Musées Royaux des Beaux-Arts de Belgique, Brussels.
Bequest of Irène Scutenaire-Hamoir, 1996, inv. 11675

> *The Daring Sleeper* (*Le Dormeur téméraire*), 1928. Oil on canvas, 115.6 x 81.3 cm.
Tate, London

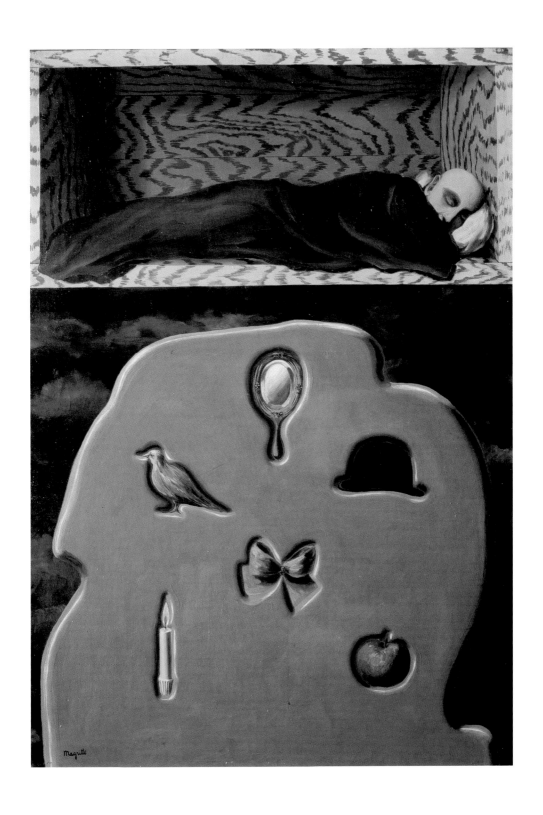

∧ *Let Out of School* (*La Sortie de l'école*), 1927. Oil on canvas, 73 x 100 cm.
Private collection, Switzerland

< *The Finery of the Storm* (*La Parure de l'orage*), 1927. Oil on canvas, 81 x 116 cm.
Private collection

∧ *The Flowers of the Abyss I* (*Les Fleurs de l'abîme I*), 1928. Oil on canvas, 54 x 73 cm.
Private collection, Belgium

< *The Flowers of the Abyss II* (*Les Fleurs de l'abîme II*), 1928. Oil on canvas, 41 x 27 cm.
Private collection

The Hunters at the Edge of Night (*Les Chasseurs au bord de la nuit*), 1928.
Oil on canvas, 81 x 116 cm. Private collection

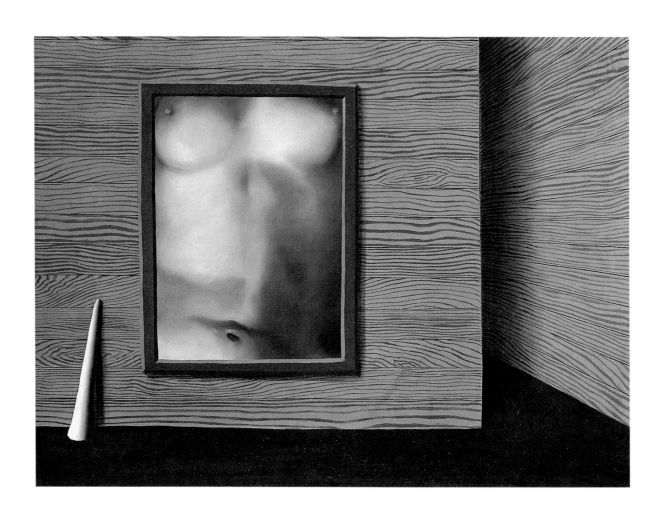

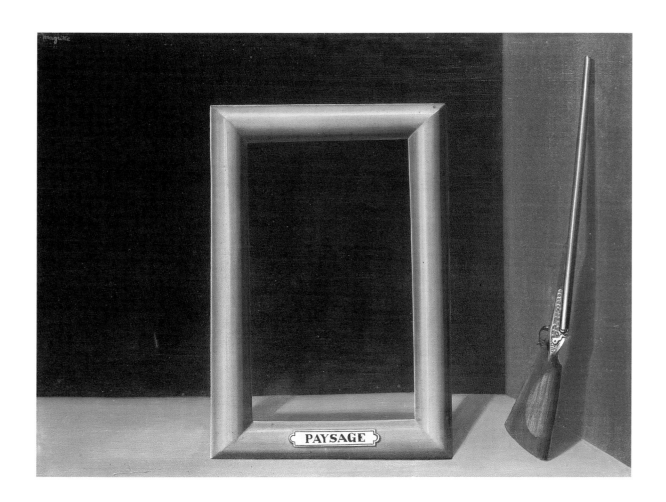

∧ *The Delights of Landscape* (*Les Charmes du paysage*), 1928. Oil on canvas, 54 x 73 cm.
Private collection

< *A Courtesan's Palace* (*Le Palais d'une courtisane*), 1928. Oil on canvas, 54 x 73 cm.
The Menil Collection, Houston

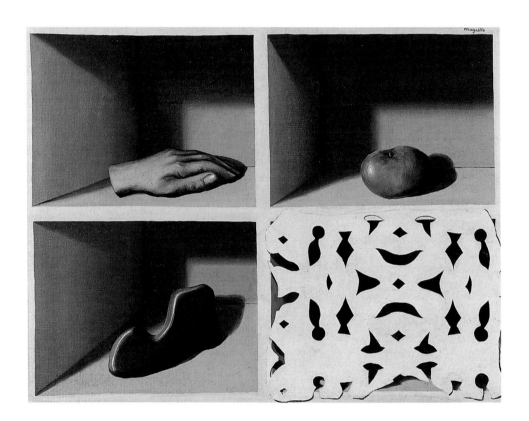

∧ *One-Night Museum* (*Le Musée d'une nuit*), 1927. Oil on canvas, 50 x 65 cm.
Private collection

> *The Man with the Newspaper* (*L'Homme au journal*), 1928. Oil on canvas, 115.6 x 81.3 cm.
Tate, London. Presented by the Friends of the Tate Gallery, 1964

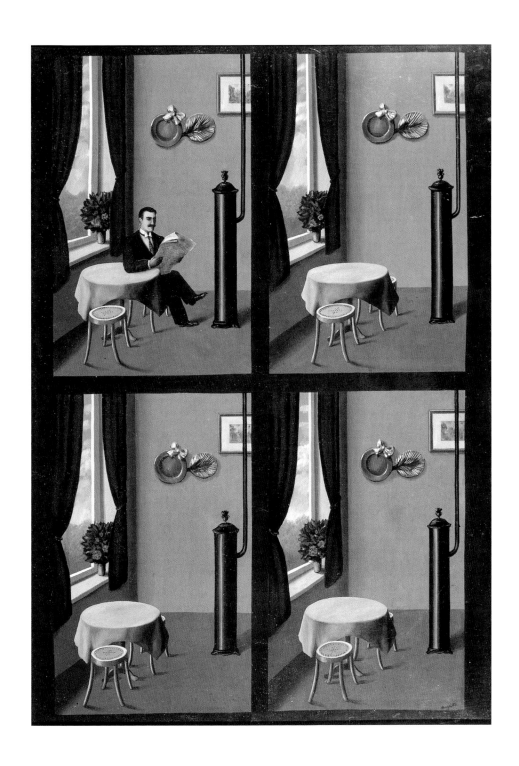

∧ *The Use of Speech* (*L'Usage de la parole*), 1928. Oil on canvas, 73 x 54 cm.
Collection Anne-Marie Martin

< *The Phantom Landscape* (*Le Paysage fantôme*), 1928. Oil on canvas, 73 x 54 cm.
Private collection, courtesy Massimo Martino Fine Arts & Projects

84

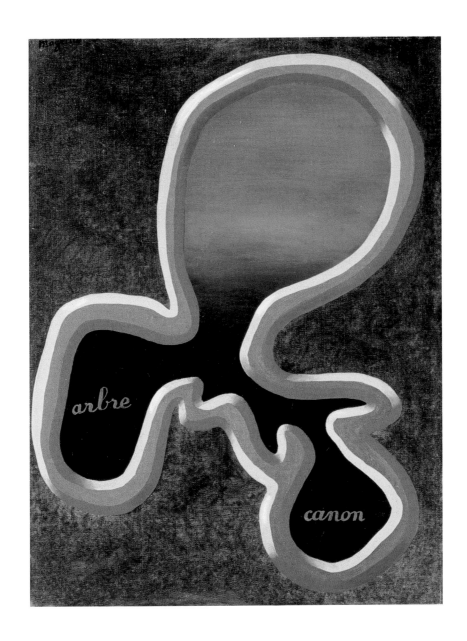

∧ *The Blue Body* (*Le Corps bleu*), 1928. Oil on canvas, 73 x 54 cm.
  Private collection

< *The Light-Breaker* (*Le Brise-Lumière*), 1927. Oil on canvas, 50 x 65 cm.
  Private collection, Switzerland

∧ *The Magic Mirror* (*Le Miroir magique*), 1929. Oil on canvas, 73 x 54 cm.
Scottish National Gallery of Modern Art, Edinburgh

< *The Literal Meaning IV* (*Le Sens propre IV*), 1929. Oil on canvas, 73 x 54 cm.
The Robert Rauschenberg Foundation Collection

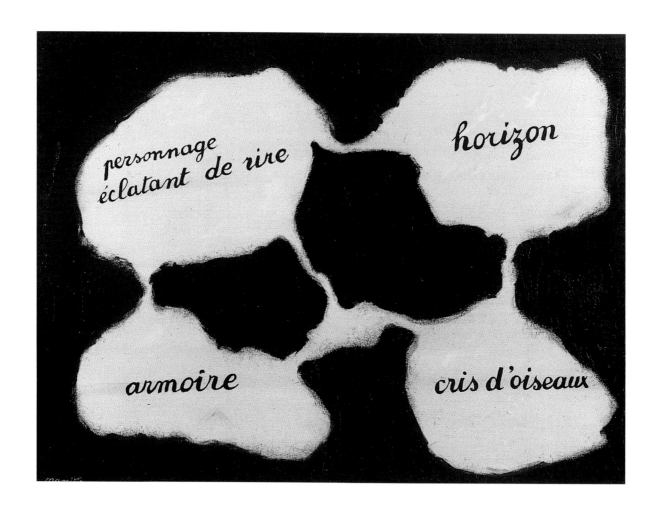

∧ *The Living Mirror* (*Le Miroir vivant*), 1928. Oil on canvas, 54 x 73 cm.
Private collection

> *The Tree of Knowledge* (*L'Arbre de la science*), 1929. Oil on canvas, 41 x 27 cm.
Private collection

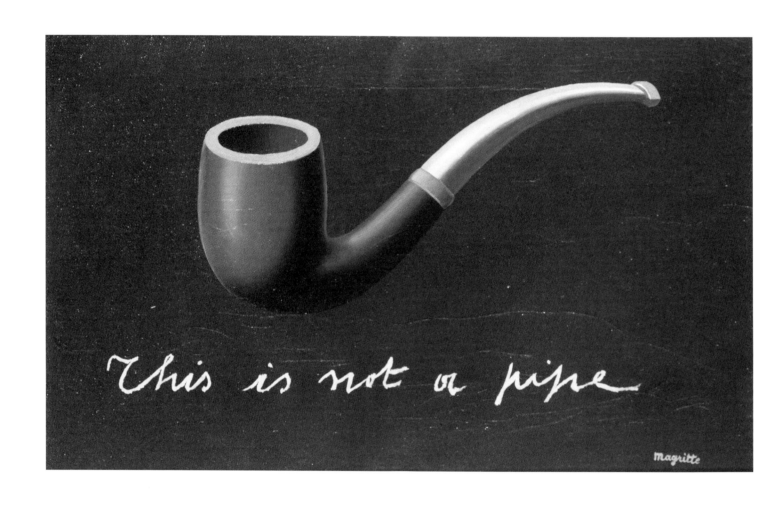

Ceci n'est pas une pipe.

Magritte

∧ *The Treachery of Images* (*La Trahison des images*), 1929. Oil on canvas, 60 x 81 cm.
  Los Angeles County Museum of Art

< *The Treachery of Images* (*La Trahison des images*), 1935. Oil on canvas, 27 x 41 cm.
  Courtesy Galerie Isy Brachot, Brussels

The Titanic Days (*Les Jours gigantesques*), 1928. Oil on canvas, 116 x 81 cm.
Kunstsammlung Nordrhein-Westfalen, Düsseldorf

∧ *The Subjugated Reader* (*La Lectrice soumise*), 1928. Oil on canvas, 92 x 73 cm.
  Ivor Braka Ltd., London

< *Figure Brooding on Madness* (*Personnage méditant sur la folie*), 1928. Oil on canvas, 54 x 73 cm.
  Musées Royaux des Beaux-Arts de Belgique, Brussels, inv. 11680

∧ *The Lovers* (*Les Amants*), 1928. Oil on canvas, 54 x 73 cm.
Private collection

< *The Lovers* (*Les Amants*), 1928. Oil on canvas, 54 x 73 cm.
Australian National Gallery, Canberra

∧ *The Symmetrical Trick* (*La Ruse symétrique*), 1928. Oil on canvas, 54 x 73 cm.
Private collection, Switzerland

< *The Invention of Life* (*L'Invention de la vie*), 1928. Oil on canvas, 81 x 116 cm.
Courtesy Zwirner & Wirth, New York, and Galerie Brusberg, Berlin

∧ *Threatening Weather* (*Le Temps menaçant*), 1929. Oil on canvas, 54 x 73 cm.
Scottish National Gallery of Modern Art, Edinburgh

< *The Flood* (*L'Inondation*), 1928. Oil on canvas, 73 x 54 cm.
Dexia Bank Collection

The Eternally Obvious (*L'Evidence éternelle*), 1930. Oil on 5 canvases,
framed and mounted on Plexiglas: 22 x 12 cm, 19 x 24 cm, 27 x 19 cm,
22 x 16 cm, 22 x 12 cm. The Menil Collection, Houston

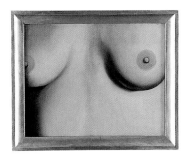

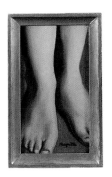

∧ *The Fair Captive* (*La Belle Captive*), 1931. Oil on canvas, 38 x 55 cm.
Hogarth Galleries, Sydney, on deposit at the Art Gallery of New South Wales, Sydney

< *The Depths of the Earth* (*Profondeurs de la Terre*), 1930. Oil on 4 canvases, framed and mounted
on glass, 12 x 22 cm, 16 x 22 cm, 22 x 16 cm, 19 x 24 cm.
Private collection

∧ *Lady of the Night* (*La Belle de nuit*), 1932. Oil on canvas, 81 x 116 cm.
Diane S.A.

< *Black Magic* (*La Magie noire*), 1934. Oil on canvas, 73 x 54 cm.
Private collection

∧ *The Rape* (*Le Viol*), 1934. Oil on canvas, 73 x 54 cm.
 The Menil Collection, Houston

< *Love Disarmed* (*L'Amour désarmé*), 1935. Oil on canvas, 72 x 54 cm.
 Private collection

∧ *Perpetual Motion* (*Le Mouvement perpétuel*), 1935. Oil on canvas, 54 x 73 cm.
Private collection, Switzerland

< *The Red Model* (*Le Modèle rouge*), 1935. Oil on canvas, 72 x 48.5 cm.
Moderna Museet, Stockholm

The Palace of Curtains (*Le Palais des rideaux*), 1935. Oil on canvas, 27 x 41 cm.
Micky and Pierre Alechinsky Collection

The *Interpretation of Dreams* (*La Clef des songes*), 1927. Oil on canvas, 38 x 55 cm.
Staatsgalerie moderner Kunst, Munich, Theo Wormland Collection

> The *Interpretation of Dreams* (*La Clef des songes*), 1935. Oil on canvas, 41 x 27 cm.
Jasper Johns Collection, New York

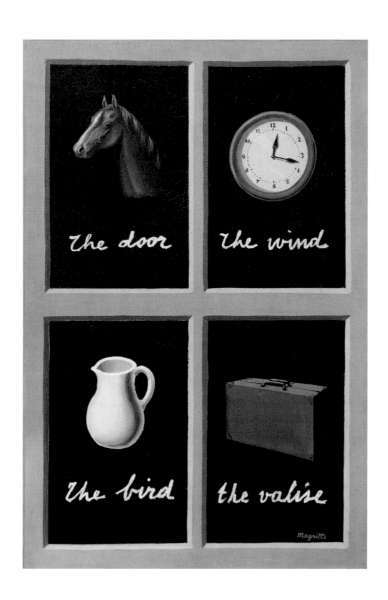

∧ *The Fair Captive* (*La Belle Captive*), 1948. Oil on canvas, 54 x 65 cm.
Private collection

< *The Discovery of Fire* (*La Découverte du feu*), 1934–5. Oil on canvas, 33 x 41 cm.
Leslee and David Rogath Collection

∧ *The Future (L'Avenir)*, 1936. Oil on canvas, 54 x 65 cm.
Private collection, Switzerland

< *This Is a Piece of Cheese (Ceci est un morceau de fromage)*, 1952. Gouache on paper, 17.5 x 15 cm.
Private collection

This Is a Piece of Cheese (Ceci est un morceau de fromage), 1936. Oil on canvas board in gilded
wooden frame, glass dome and pedestal; canvas: 14 x 18.2 cm; dome: height 35 cm,
diameter 31.5 cm. Private collection

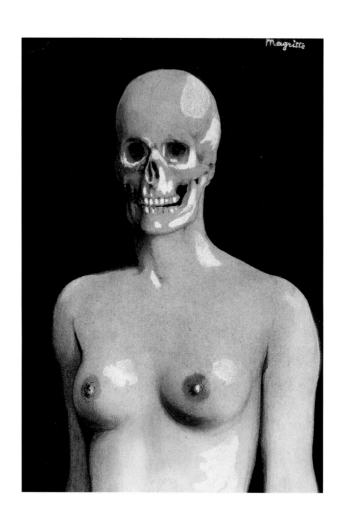

∧ *Clairvoyance* (*La Clairvoyance*), 1936. Oil on canvas, 54 x 65 cm.
   Private collection, courtesy Galerie Isy Brachot, Brussels

< *The Spoiler* (*La Gâcheuse*), 1935. Gouache, watercolor and pencil
   on tinted paper, 20.1 x 13.6 cm. Scottish National Gallery of
   Modern Art, Edinburgh. Bequest of Gabrielle Keiller

∧ *Time Transfixed* (*La Durée poignardée*), 1938. Oil on canvas, 146 x 97 cm.
   The Art Institute of Chicago, Joseph Winterbotham Collection

> *On the Threshold of Freedom* (*Au Seuil de la liberté*), 1937. Oil on canvas, 258 x 190 cm.
   The Art Institute of Chicago

∧ *The Traveler* (*Le Voyageur*), 1937. Oil on canvas, 54 x 65 cm.
Private collection

< *Youth Illustrated* (*La Jeunesse illustrée*), 1937. Oil on canvas, 183 x 136 cm.
Museum Boijmans Van Beuningen, Rotterdam

∧ *Not To Be Reproduced* (*La Reproduction interdite*), 1937. Oil on canvas, 81 x 65 cm.
   Museum Boijmans Van Beuningen, Rotterdam

< *The Pleasure Principle* (*Le Principe du plaisir*), 1937. Oil on canvas, 73 x 54 cm.
   Private collection

The Domain of Arnheim (*Le Domaine d'Arnheim*), 1938.
Oil on canvas, 73 x 100 cm. Diane S.A.

The Call of the Peaks (*L'Appel des cimes*), 1943. Oil on canvas, 65 x 54 cm.
Private collection

∧ *The Lost Jockey* (*Le Jockey perdu*), 1942. Gouache on paper, 50.5 x 65 cm.
Private collection

< *The Lost Jockey* (*Le Jockey perdu*), 1942. Oil on canvas, 60 x 73 cm.
Private collection

∧ *The Companions of Fear* (*Les Compagnons de la peur*), 1942.
 Gouache on paper, 33 x 48.5 cm.
 Musées Royaux des Beaux-Arts de Belgique, Brussels, inv. 11678

> *The Misanthropes* (*Les Misanthropes*), 1942. Oil on canvas, 54 x 73 cm.
 Hiroshima Prefectural Art Museum

∧ *The Anatomy Lesson* (*La Leçon d'anatomie*), 1943. Oil on canvas, 60 x 73 cm.
Private collection

> *The Flame Rekindled* (*Le Retour de flamme*), 1943. Oil on canvas, 65 x 50 cm.
Private collection

138

∧ *Common Sense* (*Le Bon Sens*), 1945. Oil on canvas, 48 x 78.5 cm.
Private collection, courtesy Nancy Whyte Fine Arts, Inc.

< *The First Day* (*Le Premier Jour*), 1943. Oil on canvas, 60.5 x 55.5 cm.
Private collection

∧ *A Stroke of Luck* (*La Bonne Fortune*), 1945. Oil on canvas, 60 x 80 cm.
  Musées Royaux des Beaux-Arts de Belgique, Brussels. Bequest
  of Irène Scutenaire-Hamoir, 1996, inv. 11689

< *Lyricism* (*Le Lyrisme*), 1947. Oil on canvas, 50 x 65 cm.
  Musées Royaux des Beaux-Arts de Belgique, Brussels.
  Bequest of Irène Scutenaire-Hamoir, 1996, inv. 11693

∧ *The Cripple* (*Le Stropiat*), 1948. Oil on canvas, 59.5 x 49.5 cm.
Centre Georges Pompidou, Paris, Musée national d'Art moderne/
Centre de Création industrielle

> *Pictorial Content* (*Le Contenu pictural*), 1948. Oil on canvas, 73 x 50 cm.
Private collection

∧ *Famine* (*La Famine*), 1948. Oil on canvas, 46 x 55 cm.
Musées Royaux des Beaux-Arts de Belgique, Brussels.
Bequest of Irène Scutenaire-Hamoir, 1996, inv. 11696

> *The Stop* (*L'Etape*), 1948. Oil on canvas, 55 x 46 cm.
Private collection

145

∧ *Seasickness* (*Le Mal de mer*), 1948. Oil on canvas, 54 x 65 cm.
Private collection

> *The Psychologist* (*Le Psychologue*), 1948. Oil on canvas, 65 x 54 cm.
Private collection

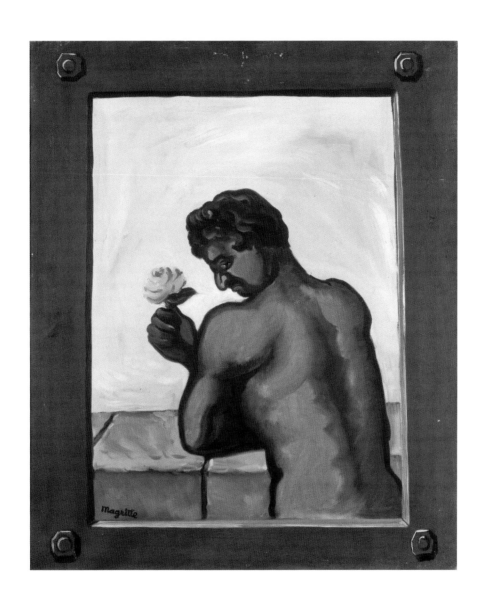

∧ *The Amorous Vista* (*La Perspective amoureuse*), 1957. Gouache on paper, 23.2 x 17.8 cm.
Private collection

> *The Healer* (*Le Thérapeute*), 1936. Gouache on paper, 47.6 x 31.3 cm.
Private collection, courtesy Guggenheim, Asher Associates, Inc.

Philosophy in the Boudoir (*La Philosophie dans le boudoir*), 1947. Oil on canvas, 80 x 60 cm.
Private collection

∧ *Good Company* (*La Bonne Compagnie*). Oil on canvas, 41.5 x 33 cm.
  Private collection

< *The Joyful Forest* (*La Forêt joyeuse*), 1948. Gouache on paper, 46.5 x 37 cm.
  Private collection, Mexico

∧ *The Smile* (*Le Sourire*), 1947. Gouache on paper, 37 x 46.2 cm.
  The Menil Collection, Houston

> *The Fissure* (*La Fissure*), 1949. Gouache on paper, 44.3 x 34.5 cm.
  Private collection

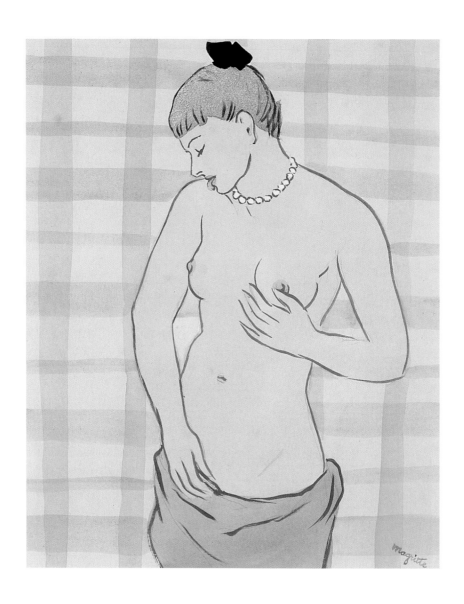

∧ *Megalomania* (*La Folie des grandeurs II*), 1948-9. Oil on canvas, 99.2 x 81.5 cm.
Hirshhorn Museum and Sculpture Garden, Smithsonian Institution,
Washington, DC. Gift of Joseph H. Hirshhorn, 1966

< *The Pebble* (*Le Galet*), 1948. Gouache on paper, 40.8 x 32.8 cm.
Musées Royaux des Beaux-Arts de Belgique, Brussels. Bequest of Irène
Scutenaire-Hamoir, 1996, inv. 11715

∧ *Elementary Cosmogony* (*Cosmogonie élémentaire*), 1949. Oil on canvas, 80 x 100 cm.
Private collection

< *The Cicerone* (*Le Cicérone*), 1948. Oil on canvas, 60 x 50 cm.
Private collection

∧ *Memory* (*La Mémoire*), 1948. Gouache on paper, 17.3 x 14.3 cm. Private collection ·

> *Memory* (*La Mémoire*), 1948. Oil on canvas, 60 x 50 cm. Collection of the Belgian State, Ministère de la Communauté française de Belgique, Service général du Patrimoine culturel et des Arts plastiques, on deposit at the Musée d'Ixelles, Brussels

∧ *The Flavor of Tears* (*La Saveur des larmes*), 1948. Oil on canvas, 60 x 50 cm.
The Barber Institute of Fine Arts, The University of Birmingham

> *The Natural Graces* (*Les Grâces naturelles*), 1948. Oil on canvas, 81 x 100 cm.
Private collection

The Haunted Castle (*Le Château hanté*), 1950. Oil on canvas, 38 x 46 cm.
Sprengel Museum, Hanover (Germany)

∧ *The Seducer* (*Le Séducteur*), 1950. Oil on canvas, 50 x 60 cm.
Virginia Museum of Fine Arts, Richmond. Mr. and Mrs. Paul Mellon
Collection, inv. 83.34

< *Scheherazade* (*Schéhérazade*), 1950. Oil on canvas, 40 x 30 cm.
Private collection, courtesy Galerie Odermatt-Vedovi, Paris

∧ *The Hesitation Waltz* (*La Valse Hésitation*), 1950. Oil on canvas, 35 x 46 cm.
   Leslee and David Rogath Collection

< *The Art of Conversation* (*L'Art de la conversation*), 1950. Oil on canvas, 50 x 60 cm.
   Private collection, Antwerp

The Magician (*Le Sorcier*), 1951. Oil on canvas, 35 x 46 cm.
Private collection, Switzerland

∧ *Perspective: David's Madame Récamier* (*Perspective: Mme Récamier de David*), 1950.
Oil on canvas, 60 x 80 cm.
Private collection, courtesy Guggenheim, Asher Associates, Inc.

> *David's Madame Récamier* (*Mme Récamier de David*), 1967. Bronze, 197 x 196 x 50 cm.
Centre Georges Pompidou, Paris, Musée national d'Art moderne/
Centre de Création industrielle

∧ *Perspective: Gérard's Mme Récamier* (*Perspective: Mme Récamier de Gérard*), 1950.
  Oil on canvas, 65 x 50 cm. Private collection

> *Perspective: Manet's Balcony* (*Perspective: le Balcon de Manet II*), 1950.
  Oil on canvas, 80 x 60 cm. Museum voor Schone Kunsten, Ghent

The Survivor (*Le Survivant*), 1950. Gouache on paper, 46 x 36.8 cm.
Private collection, Switzerland

∧ *Memory of a Journey III* (*Souvenir de voyage III*), 1951. Oil on canvas, 80 x 65 cm.
Private collection, New York

< *The Song of the Violet* (*Le Chant de la violette*), 1951. Oil on canvas, 100 x 80 cm.
Private collection

∧ *The Art of Conversation IV* (*L'Art de la conversation IV*), 1950. Oil on canvas, 65 x 81 cm.
Private collection, Switzerland

< *The Legend of the Centuries* (*La Légende des siècles*), 1950. Oil on canvas, 55 x 46 cm.
Private collection

∧ *The Good Example* (*Le Bon Exemple*), 1953. Oil on canvas,
46.5 x 35.5 cm. Centre Georges Pompidou, Paris, Musée
national d'Art moderne/Centre de Création industrielle

> *Golconda* (*Golconde*), 1953. Oil on canvas, 80.7 x 100.6 cm.
The Menil Collection, Houston

∧ *The Dominion of Light* (*L'Empire des lumières*), 1961. Oil on canvas, 114 x 146 cm.
Private collection

< *The Dominion of Light* (*L'Empire des lumières*), 1954. Oil on canvas, 146 x 114 cm.
Mr. and Mrs. Ahmet Ertegün Collection

The Dominion of Light (*L'Empire des lumières*), 1953-4. Oil on canvas, 195.4 x 131.2 cm. Peggy Guggenheim Collection, Venice. Solomon R. Guggenheim Foundation, New York

∧ *The Masterpiece or the Mysteries of the Horizon* (*Le Chef d'œuvre ou les mystères de l'horizon*), 1955.
Oil on canvas, 50 x 65 cm. Frederick R. Weisman Art Foundation, Los Angeles

< *Memory of a Journey* (*Souvenir de voyage*), 1955. Gouache on paper, 37 x 30.5 cm.
Private collection, Mexico

∧ *The Ready-Made Bouquet* (*Le Bouquet tout fait*), 1956. Oil on canvas, 60 x 50 cm.
Private collection, Switzerland

< *The Orphan Boy* (*Sans famille*), 1958. Oil on canvas, 75 x 55 cm.
Private collection, Geneva, courtesy Galerie Daniel Varenne, Geneva

The Alarm Clock (*Le Réveille-Matin*), 1957. Oil on canvas, 50 x 60 cm.
Private collection, courtesy Galerie Isy Brachot, Brussels

∧ *Where Euclid Walked* (*Les Promenades d'Euclide*), 1956. Oil on canvas, 15 x 20 cm.
Private collection, New York

> *Where Euclid Walked* (*Les Promenades d'Euclide*), 1955. Oil on canvas, 162 x 130 cm.
The Minneapolis Institute of Arts. The William Hood Dunwoody Fund

∧ *The Labors of Alexander* (*Les Travaux d'Alexandre*), ca. 1958. Gouache on paper, 20 x 25 cm.
Private collection

> *The Labors of Alexander* (*Les Travaux d'Alexandre*), 1967. Bronze, 67.5 x 145 x 102 cm.
The Menil Collection, Houston

The Sixteenth of September (*Le Seize Septembre*), 1956. Oil on canvas, 116 x 89 cm.
Koninklijk Museum voor Schone Kunsten, Antwerp

∧ *The Listening Room* (*La Chambre d'écoute*), 1958. Oil on canvas, 38 x 46 cm.
  Kunsthaus, Zurich. Walter Haefner Donation

> *The Tomb of the Wrestlers* (*Le Tombeau des lutteurs*), 1960. Oil on canvas, 89 x 116 cm.
  Private collection

202

∧ *The Golden Legend* (*La Légende dorée*), 1958. Oil on canvas, 97 x 130 cm.
Leslee and David Rogath Collection

< *The Month of the Grape-Harvest* (*Le Mois des vendanges*), 1959.
Oil on canvas, 130 x 162 cm. Private collection

∧ *The Battle of the Argonne* (*La Bataille de l'Argonne*), 1964. Gouache on paper, 29 x 41 cm.
 Private collection

> *The Familiar World* (*Le Monde familier*), 1958. Oil on canvas, 50 x 60 cm.
 Private collection, Mexico

∧ *The Masked Ball* (*Le Bal masqué*), 1958. Oil on canvas, 60 x 50 cm.
Private collection, Switzerland

> *The Castle in the Pyrenees* (*Le Château des Pyrénées*), 1959.
Oil on canvas, 200.3 x 145 cm.
The Israel Museum, Jerusalem. Gift of Harry Torczyner

The Heartstring (*La Corde sensible*), 1960. Oil on canvas, 114 x 146 cm.
Private collection, Belgium

∧ *Mona Lisa* (*La Joconde*), 1960. Oil on canvas, 70 x 50 cm.
Private collection

< *Mona Lisa* (*La Joconde*), 1967. Bronze, 248 x 177 x 99.5 cm.
Private collection

∧ *The Curse* (*La Malédiction*), 1960. Oil on canvas, 33 x 41 cm.
Private collection, Belgium

> *The Memoirs of a Saint* (*Les Mémoires d'un saint*), 1960. Oil on canvas, 80 x 100 cm.
The Menil Collection, Houston

∧ *The Anger of the Gods* (*La Colère des dieux*), 1960.
    Oil on canvas, 61 x 50 cm. Gunter Sachs Collection

< *A Little of the Outlaws' Souls* (*Un peu de l'âme des bandits*), 1960.
    Oil on canvas, 65 x 50 cm. Private collection

Force of Habit (*La Force de l'habitude*), 1960. Oil on canvas, 61 x 50 cm.
Private collection

∧ *The Natural Graces* (*Les Grâces naturelles*), 1961. Oil on canvas, 81 x 100 cm.
Private collection

> *The Waterfall* (*La Cascade*), 1961. Oil on canvas, 81 x 100 cm.
Private collection, Switzerland

Blood Will Tell (*La Voix du sang*), 1961. Oil on canvas, 90 x 110 cm.
Private collection

∧ *Reconnaissance Without End* (*La Reconnaissance infinie*), 1963.
Oil on canvas, 81 x 100 cm. Leslee and David Rogath Collection

< *The Great Family* (*La Grande Famille*), 1963. Oil on canvas, 100 x 81 cm.
Utsunomiya Museum of Art, Utsunomiya City, Tochigi

∧ *The Man in the Bowler Hat* (*L'Homme au chapeau melon*), 1964.
   Oil on canvas, 65 x 50 cm. Private collection, New York

> *The Son of Man* (*Le Fils de l'homme*), 1964. Oil on canvas, 116 x 89 cm.
   Private collection

∧ *The Chorus of the Sphinxes* (*Le Chœur des sphinges*), 1964.
Gouache on paper, 40.5 x 29 cm. Private collection

> *The Princes of Autumn* (*Les Princes de l'automne*), 1963.
Oil on canvas, 100 x 81 cm. Private collection

∧ *Evening Falls* (*Le soir qui tombe*), 1964. Oil on canvas, 162 x 130 cm.
The Menil Collection, Houston

< *The Field-Glass* (*La Lunette d'approche*), 1963. Oil on canvas, 175.5 x 116 cm.
The Menil Collection, Houston

∧ *Carte Blanche* (*Le Blanc-Seing*), 1965. Oil on canvas, 81.3 x 65.1 cm.
National Gallery of Art, Washington, DC. Mr. and Mrs. Paul
Mellon Collection

< *The Latest Thing* (*Le Dernier Cri*), 1967. Oil on canvas, 81 x 65 cm.
Private collection

Photomontage of sixteen mugshots surrounding Magritte's *The Hidden Woman* (*Je ne vois pas la [femme] cachée dans la forêt*), as published in *La Révolution surréaliste*, no. 12, December 15, 1929. Top row, from left to right: Maxime Alexandre, Louis Aragon, André Breton, Luis Buñuel, Jean Caupenne; second row: Salvador Dalí and Paul Eluard; third: Max Ernst and Marcel Fourrier; fourth: Camille Goemans and Magritte; bottom row: Paul Nougé, Georges Sadoul, Yves Tanguy, André Thirion, Albert Valentin

Jean-Michel Goutier

The Great Semantic Bridge

When, in his interviews with André Parinaud (1952), André Breton talks about the object's place in Surrealism and especially the creation of Surrealist objects, he naturally begins with Marcel Duchamp's readymades and *Why Not Sneeze, Rrose Sélavy?* But he also brings up his own idea of executing and circulating objects perceived in dreams, like the book described in his *Introduction au discours sur le peu de réalité* (*Introduction to the Discourse on the Paucity of Reality*, 1927), as well as the constructions of Alberto Giacometti and the symbolically functional objects of Salvador Dalí. This capsule history and his definition of the *poème-objet* (object-poem) enable Breton to situate René Magritte's place within the "movement" quite precisely and, at the same time, underscore the complementary nature of their respective approaches. From their similarly configured attitudes in regard to the poetic image and the visual image, we can understand why, despite temporary interruptions, the current never ceased to flow between them, from 1927, the year they met in Paris, until 1965, the year of "L'Ecart absolu,"[1] the last International Surrealist Exhibition organized during Breton's lifetime.

"I defined the object-poem as a composition that tends to combine the resources of poetry and visual art by speculating on their power of reciprocal exaltation. Magritte—who had set out from the visual, whereas I set out from poetry—was on the lookout for what could result from the placing of highly resonant concrete words (the word "mountain," the word "pipe," the words "head of a child") in relationship to forms that repudiate them or, at least, do not correspond to them rationally."[2]

I am most grateful to Mme. Aube Elléouët-Breton for allowing me to consult, and quote excerpts from, the correspondence of André Breton and René Magritte.

1 "L'Ecart absolu," Eleventh International Exhibition of Surrealism, inaugurated December 7, 1965, at the Galerie de L'Œil, under Georges Bernier.
2 André Breton, *Entretiens* (Paris: Gallimard, 1952), p. 162.
3 In 1925, Marcel Lecomte had introduced Magritte to Giorgio de Chirico's *Song of Love* and French Surrealist poetry.
4 André Breton, *Point du jour* (Paris: Gallimard, 1934), pp. 88–89.

Before turning to the salient rapprochements and estrangements that characterized this friendship, it seems to make sense to recall two events that shed light on the friction between the various modernist currents during the 1920s: Francis Picabia's vehement indictment of Breton in 1924, in the nineteenth issue of *391* (the same issue in which some aphorisms by Magritte were published); and the expulsion on July 21, 1925 of Marcel Lecomte[3]—the first in the history of Surrealism—which was the decision of the founders of the Belgian magazine *Correspondance* and not some edict issued by Breton. Having been exposed to the settling of scores via magazines very early on, Breton and Magritte had no reason, *a priori*, to fear the inevitable heated exchanges of fire between personalities waging the same combat for the cause of liberty.

When Magritte lived in Le Perreux-sur-Marne, he regularly attended the meetings of Breton's group. But if he took up with the poets more readily than the painters, except Arp, none of them produced a text in his support; and though he rated three lines in Aragon's *La Peinture au défi* (Painting under Fire) in 1930, he was missing from the first edition of Breton's *Le Surréalisme et la peinture* (Surrealism and Painting) in 1928, for the simple reason that the manuscript had been submitted to Gallimard towards the middle of the previous year and sent on to the printer well before Breton had met the spokesman of Belgian Surrealism. The vexation, albeit unjustified, Magritte no doubt felt at this was aggravated by his unsung arrival in the group, which bears no comparison with the triumphal welcome given Dalí, of whom Breton wrote almost immediately thereafter, "With Dalí, the windows of the mind have perhaps been opened wide for the first time."[4]

On December 15, 1929, with the publication of the twelfth and last issue of *La Révolution surréaliste*, Magritte finally had the opportunity to present a masterful overview of the creative possibilities that instantly ensured him one of the brightest spots in the "movement's" constellation of painters. That issue opens with Breton's "Second Surrealist Manifesto" and concludes pyrotechnically with another, collective manifesto composed of the answers to the famous survey on love, for which Magritte made the page layout that included his canvas *Je ne vois pas la [femme] cachée dans la forêt* (*I Do Not See the [Woman] Hidden in the Forest*) framed by sixteen mugshots of Surrealists with their eyes shut. Magritte also contributed "Les Mots et les images," eighteen statements connecting poetry and visual art that form an ingenious little introductory treatise to his own painting. Breton referred repeatedly to this piece in his letters to the creator of *The Treachery of Images* (*La Trahison des images*, 1929). On April 8, 1936, for example, he wrote his friend announcing the upcoming appearance of a new magazine:

> "For your part, could you not provide a *theoretically regular contribution* (I have in mind the text of yours illustrated with drawings that appeared in No. 12 of the *R.S.*, which I had reproduced in the Surrealist issue of *Konkretion*, in Copenhagen.)"[5]

In mid-December 1929, an incident occurred that was given considerable play in the press hostile to Breton. It seems that, to the great displeasure of right-minded people, he had allowed himself to make a disapproving remark to Georgette Magritte for wearing a cross around her neck—something that was exceedingly out of place in that fiercely anticlerical milieu. But Magritte's return to Belgium with his wife in July 1930, six months after the altercation, was in actuality far more motivated by the economic crisis of 1929, the cancellation of the contract that bound him to the Galerie Le Centaure in Brussels and the closing of the Galerie Goemans in Paris than by Breton's vocal outbursts. Two years later, on July 11, 1932, Magritte acknowledged receiving a book Breton had sent, his *Revolver à cheveux blancs* (The White-Haired Revolver).

> "I am reading your book with great interest. In the first piece, I find the distinction between reality and imagination surpassed by a more remarkable view of things: the vision that responds to a secret desire, nothing absolutely prevents it from being realized."[6]

In May 1933, the fifth issue of *Le Surréalisme au service de la révolution*, of which Breton was the editor, published an excerpt from Paul Nougé's essay on Magritte, "Les Images défendues" (Forbidden Images), and from December of that year until 1935, beginning with the publication of a booklet on Violette Nozière (the schoolgirl who had been arrested for the murder of her father and the attempted murder of her mother), a great flurry of Surrealist activity took place in Brussels. Breton's lecture "Qu'est-ce que le surréalisme?" (What Is Surrealism?), given on June 1, 1934, was issued as a booklet with a picture by Magritte, *The Rape* (*Le Viol*), on the cover. And that month, in parallel with his taking part in the "Minotaure" exhibition at the Palais des Beaux-Arts, Magritte published his text "Le Fil d'Ariane" (The Thread of Ariadne) in the opening pages of the first issue of *Documents 34*, between a poem by Eluard and Breton's "Equation de l'objet trouvé" (Equation of the Found Object). A month later, Breton wrote to thank Magritte for sending him a drawing he was enthusiastic about, adding:

> "We absolutely must find some means or other of making it easier for the public to understand your most recent explorations, the importance of which, I repeat, seems to me vital. I have in fact thought of writing about it, either separately, as I did for Giacometti in *Documents 34*, or for the new edition of *Le Surréalisme et la peinture*, which is to come out this fall."[7]

Unfortunately, this new edition was not published on the projected date, and Magritte would have to wait another twenty years for a preface by Breton, aside from the notice in question-and-answer format that appeared in November 1934 in the second issue of *Documents 34*, part of which was reused to define the painter in the *Dictionnaire abrégé du surréalisme* (Concise Dictionary of Surrealism), published by the Galerie Beaux-Arts on the occasion of the International Surrealist Exhibition in 1938:

> "What is Surrealism?
> "It is the cuckoo's egg laid in the nest (the brood being lost) with the complicity of René Magritte."

A distant echo of Picabia's diatribe against Breton in *391* may be detected in this brief passage, if we consider it in light of Picabia's remark: "'Hard boiled eggs' come

5 André Breton, letter to René Magritte, April 8, 1936.
6 Magritte to Breton, July 11, 1932.
7 Breton to Magritte, July 1, 1934.

out of chicks, and I hope, my dear Breton, that you are not too disappointed by how your brood turns out." Did the founder of Surrealism bear an unconscious grudge against Magritte for having contributed to that *last* issue of the Dadaist review, before absolving himself with his dazzling contribution to the *last* issue of *La Révolution surréaliste*? At any rate, "the cuckoo's egg" is an inspired touch to describe Magritte's "estrangement."

In August 1935, bringing the intense collaboration between Belgian and French Surrealists to a close, the third issue of the *Bulletin international du surréalisme* was published, again in Brussels and under the aegis of the Belgian Surrealist group. The cover illustration was a gouache by Magritte, *The Spoiler* (*La Gâcheuse*); the review's contents comprised a collective declaration by the Belgian Surrealists, "Le Couteau dans la plaie" (The Knife in the Wound), and the entirety of Breton's "Défense de la culture," a speech delivered to a congress of the Ecrivains pour la Défense de la Culture.

Nineteen thirty-six was a pivotal year in the interchanges between Breton and Magritte. From then on, Breton regularly consulted his friend concerning exhibitions in preparation and increasingly involved him in current projects. This was especially true of the "Exposition surréaliste d'objets" (Surrealist Exhibition of Objects) at Charles Ratton's gallery, which Breton was working on in April. In a long, detailed and highly technical letter, he informs Magritte that the objects he sent have just arrived and declares how important he finds them, as well as his "absolute adherence to the spirit animating them."[8] Although Magritte never subscribed to automatism or took a stand in favor of the "interior model," he had always been fascinated by the object, and for Breton, Magritte's poetic statements held an undeniably high place in the genesis of the Surrealist object. In the same letter, Breton also requested "ten important paintings, preferably spanning a period of several years"[9] for the London exhibition.

In 1937, Breton contemplated organizing a solo exhibition of Magritte's work at the short-lived Galerie Gradiva and writing a preface for it, but the project ran

aground when a host of difficulties led to closing the space designed by Marcel Duchamp.

Exiled in the United States during World War II, Breton did not forget his promise to Magritte in 1934 of giving him a place in the new edition of *Le Surréalisme et la peinture*. He honored his commitment by reprinting "Artistic Genesis and Perspective of Surrealism," from 1941, as a chapter in the book, where Magritte's paintings are characterized as a "unique and uncompromising enterprise on the confines of the physical and the mental," and by choosing a reproduction of a new version of the 1935 painting *The Red Model* (*Le Modèle rouge*) for the cover of the Brentano's edition.

Breton's return to Paris in 1946 coincided with Magritte's incursion into Renoir territory with "sunlit Surrealism," which sparked the most serious crisis between the two men. Forgetting the French Surrealists' misadventures with the Communist Party between 1927 and 1935, at the end of the War, Magritte thought it fitting to revive the experience by joining the Belgian Communist Party. In order to precipitate the arrival of a brighter future, the rigorous theoretician of "Les Mots et les images" revamped his palette and his vocabulary, substituting the words "charm, pleasure and objects of desire" for "sadness, tedium and menacing objects." But after this feat of conjuring misfired and, in the face of a stubborn lack of understanding on the part of the Stalinist cultural authorities, Magritte returned to his customary manner, which, for that matter, he had not entirely abandoned. Breton's disappointment in the face of this raging blaze was great, and his reaction was stinging, as this excerpt from an often-quoted letter of August 14, 1946 shows:

"My dear friend,
I do not know if my letter was conventional (however I did not mean it to be), but yours is of a bitterness … sweeter [to you] than to children. Why attack your friends of former times with such frenzy, on the pretext that the grace you claim to spread has not yet touched them any more than me? Indeed, there is nothing very solar about that, I think. You will end up convincing me that you have no sun within you. And how can it be, since you feel the need to look for the sun in Renoir? You go looking for it there but it doesn't follow you and, besides, Magritte's sun would, by definition, be different."[10]

8 Breton to Magritte, April 8, 1936. See note 2.
9 *Ibid*.
10 José Pierre, *Magritte* (Paris: Somogy, 1984), pp. 127-128. English translation partly quoted from *René Magritte. Catalogue raisonné*, ed. David Sylvester, vol. 2 (Houston: Menil Foundation/Antwerp: Fonds Mercator, 1993), p. 133.

After the "sunlit Surrealism" campaign, Magritte took up another battle, this one completely suicidal, by experimenting with the "Vache" style, outdoing the preceding attempt, delivering the final blow to his painting and turning his first solo exhibition in Paris, at the Galerie du Faubourg in May–June 1948, into a total fiasco.

Breton soon forgot Magritte's summer storms on canvas and, so, upon the opening of the Surrealist gallery A l'Etoile scellée in 1952, he renewed friendly intercourse with his Brussels correspondent:

"I very much like the drawing you sent me; it in itself attests to what is yours and yours alone, which I have never ceased to rank very high. And *very* fine those canvases you sent me photographs of last year. You do not suspect that I have always had the highest regard for your spirit; indeed, that is why I have often been greatly distressed, you know this as well, by the tone you thought you could set for what has been, as far as I am concerned, only passing dissension between us. I deplore it when friendships that were profound, on my part at least, are swallowed up in that. So much the worse for the heart, isn't it? My way of thinking remains nonetheless drawn to yours as if by a magnet."[11]

Magritte replied by return post to Breton's proposal of December 27, 1952, asking him to contribute to the almanac of *Flair*:

"I am delighted, dear friend, to take up an activity with you again that could very well shine more brilliantly than ever, chasing the shadows away from our friendship."[12]

But despite this newly mended climate, other shadows did at times arise—almost always, it must be admitted, occasioned by a refusal of openness on the part of the painter, who viewed few of his "confrères" in the

"movement" with favor, not to mention other art currents. Breton's interest in lyrical abstraction in 1954, for example, nearly led to a new outbreak of the cold war between Brussels and Paris. Upon receiving Breton's *L'Art magique* in 1957, to which he had even contributed by answering, true enough quite ungraciously, the questionnaire it contained, Magritte wrote to Paul Colinet to tell him how little he thought of it and to point out the absence of "'abstract' paintings (while the author has shown no repugnance for these nullities)."[13] Likewise, the comments he made to Breton in a letter of October 1961 about the booklet *Le la*, a collection of ideas that occurred in periods of wakefulness, are quite ambiguous:

"*Le la* makes one desire to know many other thoughts brought by the night. The attention given these thoughts quite seems to me not to be possible unless our life is truly *taken seriously*. This *seriousness* furthermore being the only thing making it possible to give valid esteem to humor—a very specific humor."[14]

This letter to Breton must be compared with another that Magritte had written to Gaston Puel on 8 March 1955, in which he declares, "Like you, I find Breton a bit depressing. He is no longer seeking the 'philosopher's stone' (did he ever?). What he is doing now seems to me set once and for all, and *very serious*. I have already noted this *seriousness* in him."[15]

Breton was not taken in by Magritte's maladroit compliments on *Le la* in the letter of 1961, compliments that in fact preceded another request for a preface. The request was granted, but not until 1964, with "Envergure de René Magritte" (The Stature of René Magritte), a text that neither the painter nor Dominique de Menil, the curator of the exhibition at the Arkansas Art Center in Little Rock, appreciated for what it was worth. He found that it overpraised the intellectual Dore Ashton; she thought it was above the heads of the American public. Breton's reply to the scarcely veiled accusations of his supposed spirit of seriousness (which were at times even less veiled: "If he was formerly the spokesman of a trend of great value to us, it is no doubt by giving what he said an irritating sense that he could say it?"[16]) was affectionate, though not devoid of irony:

"Perhaps I too am given to overestimating the powers of a certain brand of humor from the trans-

11 André Breton, letter to René Magritte, December 13, 1952.
12 Magritte to Breton, December 28, 1952.
13 Magritte to Paul Colinet, September 1957, in René Magritte, *Ecrits complets*, ed. André Blavier (Paris: Flammarion, 2001), p. 445.
14 Magritte to André Breton, October 12, 1961.
15 Magritte to Gaston Puel, March 8, 1955, in René Magritte, *Ecrits complets*, op. cit. note 13, p. 207.
16 Magritte to Mirabelle Dors and Maurice Rapin, March 7, 1956, in *Quatre-vingt-deux lettres de René Magritte à Mirabelle Dors et Maurice Rapin* (Paris 1976), p. 32.

Escaut [i.e. Belgian] (if that's what you call it?) …
That sort of humor—very particular—I *delight in it*
and at the same time it disturbs me, as I was saying
to Jane Graverol again quite recently. It disturbs
me because it tends to subordinate everything else
to it and thereby diminish poetry's chances, which
most assuredly are *also* on the side of seriousness."[17]

For all that, despite the snags, Breton and Magritte's
friendship extended over nearly forty years, and these
concluding lines from a long letter the author

of *Le Surréalisme et la peinture* sent to the painter of *Clash
of Universals* (*Querelle des universaux*, 1928)[18]—

"I was more than interested in your recent
exhibition. Even if our friendship has been stormy
at times, you must believe that I have never ceased
recognizing your genius and evaluate on a grand
scale the extent of the properties that are yours and
yours alone. Let me shake hands with you."[19]

—seem to me to reveal the lucidity of Breton. By 1929
the latter had already perceived how Magritte's putting
"the visual image systematically on trial"[20] could
dialectically strengthen his "movement," the motivating
priority of which had until then been the quest for the
"interior model." Moreover, if we keep in mind Novalis's
definition of genius—"the faculty of speaking
of imaginary objects as real objects and of treating them
as such"[21]—Breton's tribute assumes its true breadth.

17 Breton to Magritte, July 12, 1962.
18 A painting that belonged to André Breton.
19 Breton to Magritte, July 8, 1960.
20 André Breton, *Le Surréalisme et la peinture* (Paris: Gallimard, "Folio
   essais" series, 2002), p. 99; quoted in English from *Surrealism and
   Painting*, trans. Simon Watson Taylor (London: Macdonald, 1972),
   p. 72.
21 Albert Béguin, *L'Âme romantique et le rêve* (1937) (Paris: José Corti, 1939),
   p. 202.

The Literal Meaning (*Le Sens propre*), 1961. Papier collé and gouache on paper,
19 x 25 cm. Galerie Xavier Hufkens, Brussels

The Dead Bird (L'Oiseau mort), 1926. Papier collé and gouache on paper,
63.5 x 48.5 cm. Private collection

Paris, March 10, 1936

My dear friend,

Am I condemned to start all my letters to you with an apology? And yet, once again … As usual, I deeply appreciated the latest things you sent me: that drawing for the program of *Ubu enchaîné* [*Ubu Bound*] and the proposals for objects are sensational. But I have been extremely tired and feverish for some time, prey to a kind of perverse laxity. Forgive me this time, truly.

The performance of *Ubu* has been delayed owing to the indisposition of the lead actor (a replacement will no doubt be necessary). The exhibition of Surrealist objects at Ratton's will certainly come off at the end of April, and the comprehensive exhibition in London is a certainty for June. It was terribly remiss of me not to have informed you that all the photos for the catalogue of objects must be in by March 20—in ten days! Can you, and Paul Nougé and Mesens as well, do something by that date? I think I told you that this exhibition was to include proper Surrealist objects, found objects and wild, particularly irrational-looking objects. Could you provide photos of objects belonging to the second category? I am very much counting on you all for that as well.

I do not have your letter at hand to answer (the disorder I was mentioning). Whatever my faults in this instance, I ask you to do the impossible so that this event in Paris will leave nothing to be desired. You know that we are increasingly fascinated here by your work, which is an unbroken succession of discoveries (that is at any rate Dalí's opinion, Eluard's, Picasso's, it seems to me, and mine).

Can I count on you to impress upon my very dear Paul Nougé how important I consider his participation in the exhibition in question? Mesens promised me he would collaborate actively with us on this occasion. I am moreover going to remind him of it shortly.

I am carried away by the plan for a table you shared with me—no pun intended, forgive me. The problem is how to proceed with the execution of this object. Help us. We are not very industrious here and haven't a penny.

The drawings of yours that were in the exhibition at Les 4 Chemins have not yet been returned to me. This morning, I asked Eluard to retrieve them.

The issue of *Surrealismus* from Prague just came out. I am waiting for a second copy to forward to you.

Singer told me that Nougé and you were going to be on the A.R.C. committee. Finally, a good omen. The last issue of *Documents* is as covered in dust as you could wish. If possible, give me some details about this matter.

This letter is boring and written in haste, but I couldn't put it off any longer. Please give my best regards to your wife. And to you, my dear friend, with all my heart,

André Breton

First published in *Lettres mêlées*, Brussels: Les Lèvres nues, 1979, p. 36

Jette-Brussels, June 24, 1946
135 Rue Esseghem

Dear friend,

I am sending you a small painting, *Freedom of Worship* [*La Liberté des cultes*], today. I hope it arrives and that you will write and tell me. The paintings from my "sunlit period" are obviously in contrast to many of the things we were bent on before 1940. That, I believe, is the main explanation for the resistance they engender. However, I believe we no longer live to prophesy (always in an unpleasant sense, it should be noted). At the International Surrealist Exhibition in Paris, people had to make their way with flashlights. We experienced that during the Occupation, and it was no laughing matter. The confusion, the panic that Surrealism wanted to instill so that everything would be called into question, some Nazi morons achieved it much more successfully than we, and there was no getting around it. I did a painting, *The Black Flag* [*Le Drapeau noir*], that gave a foretaste of the terror that was to come from aerial bombs, and I am not proud of it. That and the need for change, which need not be upheld for "progress," seem to me to justify this "irruption" of a new atmosphere in my pictures and the desire to know it in real life. I am pitting the quest for joy and pleasure against the widespread pessimism. This joy and pleasure, which are so common and beyond our reach—it seems to me that it is entirely up to those of us who know a bit about *how feelings are invented* to make them accessible to us? It is not a question of abandoning the science of objects and feelings that Surrealism spawned, but of employing it for other ends than formerly, or else we will be bored just as stiff in Surrealist museums as in the others.

In regard to my new painting, you object, among other things, that you do not experience the physical sensation of pleasure I am attempting to cause with it. In any case, there can be no mistake about it: that is what I want to cause, and if I do not succeed, neither can one maintain with a straight face that Matta, Ernst, Brauner, etc., succeed in their aims; we also know very well what they want, even too well as far as I am concerned.

As for the reproach of imitating Renoir, there is some misunderstanding: I make paintings after Renoir, Ingres, Rubens, etc., but without using Renoir's particular technique. Rather, it is that of Impressionism—Renoir, Seurat and others included. For that matter, depending on the subject, some of my latest pictures required me to use the old technique (smooth, polished painting), but with lighter colors—severity is banished from it. THE SEVERITY IS MORE DISTANT, less measurable.

As you know, I will be having an exhibition in Paris in October. Would you be kind enough to write a preface for the catalogue? Even if you refuse to be won over by these images that are on good terms with the sun, might you be willing to explain what they are about, without taking a stand, and give these images a chance to shine?

I await your response. I was very happy to see you again and hope to see you often.

Until soon, and please accept my sincere feelings of friendship and trust.

Magritte

P.S. Don't forget the *savoir-vivre*!

Huelgoat, August 14, 1946

My dear friend,

I do not know if my letter was conventional (however I did not mean it to be), but yours
is of a bitterness … sweeter [to you] than to children. Why attack your friends of former times with
such frenzy, on the pretext that the grace you claim to spread has not yet touched them any more than
me? Indeed, there is nothing very solar about that, I think. You will end up convincing me that you
have no sun within you. And how can it be, since you feel the need to look for the sun in Renoir?
You go looking for it there but it doesn't follow you and besides Magritte's sun would, by definition,
be different. You may be sure that none of your latest canvases gives me the impression of the sun
(Renoir, yes), really not the slightest illusion. Am I to blame, after all? However, I object with all
my strength to being confined to the night and for a long time my taste has run to Watteau and
Seurat, Charles Cros and the Rimbaud of *Patience*, as well as El Greco and Kleist. Contrary to what
you think, I *too* am enamored of the light, but created light only.*

At the risk of causing you greater displeasure—and to my regret, this is not a mere stock phrase
of politeness—I would remind you what became of De Chirico the instant, perhaps for reasons
as valid as yours, he intentionally left behind his nocturnal period, or dream period, as you prefer.
It is quite amusing: didn't he flatter himself to think he had stolen Raphael's secret, copying the
backgrounds of his Virgins? What is one to do? He thought he had stepped out into the open air
one day. At last, he could breathe. And I give you two horses happily pawing the ground. You must
believe, my dear Magritte, that I harbor no particular dislike of horses: they have never thrown me,
and I tolerate them when I find them in Géricault, for example. The bad thing is that De Chirico's
horses … were not horses but comical masses of smoke and cotton vaguely constructed along the lines
of the animal. The countryside around them, or what was meant as such, was painful to see.

There you have them, the ghosts, these dummy horses, this sun with no effect! I say this to you
without fear, you who have so often succeeded in "finding something new" and rendering
it perceptible. In Huelgoat, where you quite obscurely congratulate me for being, rather than
in Duchamp's studio, I tell you it almost never stops raining—*real* rain, that is, as in Van Gogh
and a canvas by Rousseau I so admired in New York. But never mind, you get used to it!

Like you, I remain determined all the same to situate the golden age within our lifetime
—the contrary would be just a tad idiotic, wouldn't it? But as for "diverting, for the benefit—?—
of the socialist idea, the part of me that can be utilized": no, I am against that very vocabulary, which
I no longer share in (diverting, utilizing). The socialist idea, to which I remain absolutely faithful,
only stands to lose by these legalistic subtleties.

Most amicably, if it were up to me alone,

André Breton

* The sun does not necessarily bring happiness. Just go and have a look around Haiti sometime.

First published in André Breton, "5 Lettres," *En Hollande*, MMXVI; reprinted in José Pierre, *Magritte*, Paris: Somogy, 1984, pp. 127–8

August 20, 1946

My dear friend,

Perhaps it would be amusing to hit the ball endlessly back and forth. You write that "I have no sun within me," and I would answer: it is of course the "extramental" sun I am talking about, and so on. However, I believe you would grow tired of this game as quickly as I. You know, for some time now, I have had the depressing feeling that the life is seeping out through the cracks of "crystalized Surrealism" and that dramatic steps need be taken. What seemed to me the means of again righting and rejuvenating a currently inadequate mental world was this light, which is novel to us and quite overwhelming. This light, which for the time being we categorize as "solar," is to my mind the call of the extramental world, the world of external reality we live in. In comparison with De Chirico's intentions, there is some resemblance when he wanted to leave behind a period that was done with, but it is totally different when De Chirico called upon the neglected delights of Italian painting, going back to school instead of playing hooky. Not just anything can be placed in the presence of our existence and made to serve as a valid test of it (Italian art, military art and existentialism, for example, are not contradictory terms apt to make us hope for a higher synthesis).

I intend to remake a painting like *The Lonely Landscape* [*Le Paysage isolé*] (which shows a figure from the back in a *nondescript* landscape, who looks at it and says, "I see nothing around the landscape."). I would like to give the figure and the landscape the harshness, and perhaps the secret, of existence by flooding them with light. (By the way, I have no regret at abandoning one of those "fine ideas" whereby the figure would be obscured in the dazzling landscape.) The darkness of night that *we do not see* around the landscape is that which *cannot be thought, which exists beyond* our mental universe.

The colors of the painting will be the most cheerful I can possibly obtain. I will use to the best of my ability the technique perfected by those honest Impressionists, which is perfectly suited for this purpose.

Does that strike you as illegitimate? I hope soon to be able to send you a reproduction of this painting, which I think will be a sort of *coup de grâce* upon our ghosts. Your friend,

Magritte

Spirit and Form (*L'Esprit et la Forme*), 1961. Papier collé and gouache on paper, 44.5 x 36.5 cm. Private collection

Youth illustrated (*La Jeunesse illustrée*), 1936–7. Gouache on paper, 36 x 52 cm. Collection of the Belgian State, deposited at the Musée d'Art Wallon, Liège, by the Ministère de la Communauté Française de Belgique, Service Général du Patrimoine Culturel et des Arts Plastiques

Renilde Hammacher

Edward James and René Magritte, Magicians of the Surreal

I met Edward James, collector and art patron, in the early 1970s, at the time of the first Salvador Dalí exhibition in the Netherlands, scheduled in 1971.[1] James was an original fellow, exceedingly individualistic and mysterious. As I came to know him better, he proved to be a fascinating character, and, over the years, he became a very dear friend.

Edward James was born in Scotland in 1907. He had four sisters and was the only son of an upper-class English family. At his father's early death, he inherited a huge fortune and a grand estate that included West Dean House, farms and woodlands, near Chichester, in the lovely rolling valleys of West Sussex, in the south of England.

James's godfather was King Edward VII, who was a friend of his mother's and a frequent distinguished guest at West Dean House, where he took part in large hunting parties. Neither confirming nor denying the gossip that he was actually the sovereign's son, James smiled discretely and allowed it to spread. There was an obvious physical resemblance between the two men, and it amused James to emphasize it by wearing the same type of beard as the king.

At an early age, James showed an interest in the arts, as well as trees, birds and nature, and wished to do great things. But he realized that what was most important was to live and carry out his dreams. The conventional social life of the Edwardian establishment did not suit the young nonconformist. In the early 1930s, he left England for Paris, where he soon came into contact with Surrealist circles. He met artists, writers and musicians who gravitated around André Breton: Max Ernst, Joan Miró, Man Ray, Paul Eluard, Roland Penrose, Léonor Fini, Roberto Matta. He became friends with Dalí and Gala, and it is probably the Spanish artist who, about 1935-6, put him in touch with René Magritte. It was at this time that James began intense activity as an art collector and patron. Between 1935 and 1939, he built up a large collection of Dalí's best works, masterpieces of the Surrealist period. He acquired other Surrealist creations as well, but at first, it was Dalí's aggressive and sometimes morbid paranoiac-critical iconography that especially fascinated him. At the time, James's enthusiasm for Surrealism was quite exceptional in England, where this new trend from France was not at all popular or appreciated in the 1930s. Even Herbert Read was rather hostile to the movement, before agreeing to write an introduction for the 1936 International Surrealist Exhibition at the New Burlington Galleries in London (to which Edward James lent a Picasso and a Dalí).

James was a financial supporter of and contributor to the magazine *Minotaure*, which published several of his essays, including a subtly humorous piece about the queen of England's hats[2] and some poems.[3] He liked being thought of as a poet, and, even if the critics did not consider him a genius, they were intrigued by his original lifestyle, brimming with imagination and ambition in the realm of art.

In 1931 he married Tilly Lösch, a dancer from Vienna. It was a tumultuous and short-lived marriage, but it lasted long enough for James to "acquire" a series of ballets for his wife to dance the principal role in: "Les Ballets 33," for which he secured the collaboration of Kurt Weill and Bertolt Brecht. James was also interested in the Ballets Russes and was in contact with Balanchine, Stravinsky and Darius Milhaud; in addition, he was a great friend of the conductor Igor Markevich, who often visited him in London.

James's centers of interest were very diversified and extensive: painting, literature, poetry, music and dance. His architectural interventions in a number of his many houses (in London, Sussex, Amalfi, Hollywood) occupied him passionately. His more than comfortable

---

All the quotations from Edward James are from the letters held by the Edward James Foundation in West Dean.

1 I was then chief curator of the Museum Boijmans Van Beuningen in Rotterdam and curator of that exhibition.
2 "Le Chapeau du peuple, les Chapeaux de la reine," *Minotaure* (1936), no. 9, pp. 54-9.
3 "Trois Sécheresses," illustrated by Dalí, *Minotaure* (1936), no. 8.

Magritte in front of *Youth Illustrated* (*La Jeunesse illustrée*)
at Edward James's London house, 1937

material circumstances enabled him to lend his financial support to various artistic disciplines, and he did so unreservedly. Somewhat naive and overly credulous, he was at times the victim of his own generous nature.

The artist–patron relationship that developed between René Magritte and Edward James in 1937 was important for the international distribution of the Belgian painter's work. Edward James the poet was fascinated by Magritte's painting, its atmosphere being more poetic and mysterious to him than that of other Surrealists, and by the very personal poetic imagination evidenced in its vision of reality and meticulous rendering of details set in irrational contexts.

In January 1937, James invited Magritte to come and stay with him: "I would be delighted if you could come to London to spend a month or two here at No. 35 Wimpole Street." Magritte accepted the invitation and left for London without his wife, Georgette, or their little dog. He spent five weeks there, from February 12

to March 19, and gave a talk at the London Gallery, which it seems was attended by Georgette and his friends the Scutenaires. In his introduction, Magritte explained that it was less a lecture than a "demonstration of important ideas pertaining to some of the characteristics proper to words, images and real objects."

At James's Wimpole Street house, the artist had the use of a spacious studio over the garage. There he made preparatory sketches and three large paintings, his first major commission from a foreign collector. *The Red Model* (*Le Modèle rouge*)—the third version of this well-known "image" from Magritte's repertoire—was finished first. The larger second composition, *On the Threshold of Freedom* (*Au Seuil de la liberté*), transposed a painting from 1930 to a vertical format, as required by the wall it was intended for. The third, entitled *Youth Illustrated* (*La Jeunesse illustrée*), introduced a new theme into Magritte's vocabulary. (There exist a gouache and a small horizontal painting of the same subject, also dating from 1937.) Its objects and attributes—barrel, plaster female torso, recumbent lion, billiard table, tuba—became recurrent motifs, often placed in unexpected settings, as in *Homesickness* (*Le Mal du pays*), where the lion prominently occupies the foreground. (In a letter to James from 1939 that includes a sketch, Magritte already defines the painting, which was not executed until 1941, as "a form of 'sentimental' surrealist poetry.") The three large compositions were for the Adam ballroom of James's London house, where, through a two-way mirror setup, they only became visible when the mirrors were lit from behind. James was delighted with the results. He wrote to Magritte in April 1938, after a ball he had given in honor of one of his nieces, "Your paintings created a great sensation at my ball. That evening, *Youth Illustrated* prompted many conversions to Surrealism among England's youth. But above all, the human boots [*The Red Model*] struck a chord in the young dancing couples with their capitalist heels!" When James left for the United States in 1939, he had the paintings from his London house transferred to a barn at West Dean House.

James had also wanted Magritte to do his portrait in 1937. The painter agreed but executed it after his return to Brussels, from a photo James sent showing him from behind, in front of *On the Threshold of Freedom*. In the portrait *Not to Be Reproduced* (*La Reproduction interdite*), James is seen from behind as well, but standing in front of a mirror that is used not to reveal his face, but to hide it from the viewer, for, against all logic, the mirror reflects the image of his back. The doubling of the figure seen from behind heightens the enigma. James wrote to Magritte that he was delighted with the portrait. In reply, the painter announced he had an idea for a second portrait to serve as its pendant, which he would call *The Pleasure Principle* (*Le Principe du plaisir*). Magritte again worked from a photo, this time taken by Man Ray, for which he specified the pose: front view, sitting at a table, right hand on the table and, at the left in front of him, a stone. Magritte did not represent James as a man "without" a face, but as a man with an "invisible" face, made unidentifiable by a gleaming light that transforms the head into a radiant ball above the shoulders and chest. He did not like standard realistic portraits or, as he called them, "total portraits." On the contrary, he prized what was "hidden" and often represented his figures with their face concealed by some object such as an apple, a flower, a bird or a bowler hat. (In a photograph by Duane Michals, he hides his own face with his hand.) His Surrealist friends referred to these works as *portraits manqués* ("failed portraits"). And so, he must have delighted in conferring an unexpected, unusual and appropriately Surrealist appearance upon

James. He himself considered the work very successful, in a word, "brilliant"!

An instinctive Surrealist and extremely individualistic, James adored these two portraits, which, as he put it, "honorably" distinguished him from ordinary mortals. He even asked Magritte for permission to use *Not to Be Reproduced* as the frontispiece for his book *Rich Man, Poor Man, Beggarman, Wop*, which he was preparing for publication.

In April 1937, Magritte announced to James, "I am starting on *The Poetic World* [*Le Monde poétique*], which is intended for you." This was the sixth and last of the oil paintings he executed at the collector's request. In May 1937, Magritte informed him that, "Your portrait from behind is finished, and *The Poetic World* as well."

During his stay in London, Magritte also executed a three-dimensional work entitled *The Future of Statues* (*L'Avenir des statues*): a plaster death mask of Napoleon, painted with a blue sky and luminous white clouds. In a letter to Georgette, he says that he intended to offer the mask to James as a thank-you for his generosity and hospitality. That explains how Napoleon found his way into the Edward James collection.

Magritte, ca. 1965. Photograph by Duane Michals

In the second half of 1937, there were no further commissions, but James bought several more important paintings and gouaches, either directly from the artist or at E. L. T. Mesens's London Gallery, where Magritte regularly exhibited. In 1939, James acquired the painting *Time Transfixed* (*La Durée poignardée*, 1938), which Magritte suggested placing at the foot of the stairs at Wimpole Street, using a drawing to make his case.

James's interest in Magritte's activity subsequently continued. He tried to stimulate the artist's creative imagination with advice, comments and warnings, as their abundant correspondence shows. Magritte seems to have particularly appreciated this input. Every time he had a new idea or began a new painting, he described it in detail to James in a letter, most often accompanied by a sketch or a drawing, "so it will be quite clear." In fact, Magritte was hoping and waiting for James to suggest—as he had with Dalí—an annual contract ceding him the entirety of his output. In July 1938, Magritte wrote quite audaciously suggesting that James pay him annually, in the month of August, a given amount in exchange for the best work of his recent production. The collector, avid to retain his independence and unwilling to commit himself into the future or take risks, answered somewhat stiffly (in a letter that was perhaps never sent): "If suddenly you were to become a bad painter—nothing is impossible"— James was thinking of De Chirico—"I would be buying the work of an 'artistic fabricator' every year rather than that of an artist." The "deal" was not accepted, but this difference did not shake their friendship or professional relations. Magritte sent a conciliatory note to James, who, having somewhat moderated the artist's illusions, invited him and his wife to take a trip to Italy with him: "This trip will do your painting even more good than selling me a painting a year."

Magritte knew he could count on James when it came to defending new initiatives, as he had occasion to confirm during the difficult War years. In 1942, he informed James that he was creating "various objects: masks, statuettes, painted bottles and other things" and announced he had obtained a commission from Paris for fifty painted bottles. In reply, James pointed out that exhibitions of Surrealist objects were always very successful in America and warmly encouraged him to pursue that prospect. "You will sell quantities of them at good prices. It is exactly the taste of New York and

Hollywood, too." He recommended several galleries that could look after his interests, such as the Julien Levy Gallery and the Pierre Matisse Gallery in New York. Magritte ended up choosing the Perls Gallery.

The James–Magritte correspondence carried on until about 1950, when James left Europe for America and turned his attention to other ambitions. About fifty letters were exchanged between them, as well as many telegrams, the telegram being James's preferred means of communication. These documents constitute a valuable source for a more in-depth study of the men's reciprocal aspirations.[4]

The importance of the role played by Edward James in Magritte's career and creative activity should not be underestimated. On the whole, insufficient attention has been paid to James's influence, which was decisive for the painter's international reputation. In an interview in 1965, Magritte willingly acknowledged that in 1937 "an Englishman … gave me a very large commission, and after that, I sold a little more every year. I sell a lot in the United States, through some major dealers."

Some years later, Edward James at last carried out one of his fondest wishes: he converted West Dean House into a socio-cultural educational center—The Edward James Foundation/West Dean College—where crafts such as musical instrument-making, tapestry weaving and the restoration of precious ceramic and porcelain wares are currently taught. But this was only an interlude. From the 1950s on, James led an increasingly nomadic life, moving from one continent to another. He became deeply attracted to Mexico and settled in Xilitla, a small village in a remote corner of the jungle, where he developed a huge, hallucinatory project, living with the indigenous population amid exotic flora and fauna. This lord of the manor, writer, poet, collector, patron of the arts, amateur architect and inventor of droll stories became the builder of an immense Surrealist dream, a "Garden of Delights" in the subtropical bush, with palaces of various styles and towers reaching toward the clouds, topped with great flowers and birds of colored stone. His cult of the bizarre and his fertile imagination blossomed profusely in Mexico, while Magritte, tranquilly pursuing his path back in his native country, confirmed his identity as a Surrealist artist.

Although he achieved wide recognition, Magritte adhered to the simple lifestyle of a modest bourgeois who did not want to be seen as out of the ordinary but

---

4 Edward James Archives, Edward James Foundation, West Dean Estate.

preferred to blend in with the crowd. He continued his work and followed his poetic and creative course in quest of the "mystery of reality," while James, in making his dreams a reality, spent a large part of his fortune and decided to sell his collection. It was dispersed to museums and private collections around the world. Interested in neither a particular social status nor wealth, he felt that he had derived great pleasure from collecting and done his duty as a patron by helping the young Surrealists. He did not wish to hold a monopoly on his privileged situation.

At the end of his life, he looked like a figure from the Bible, a bearded prophet living in a wild, prehistoric landscape. He was nicknamed "Jungle James," and, to him, this title was the most flattering he had ever been accorded, other than poet. At his request, his tombstone in the park at West Dean is engraved simply: *Edward James 1907-1984—Poet*.

Edward James with Abraham Hammacher at West Dean House, 1975

May 18, 1937

My dear friend,

I was most delighted by your telegram: to know that my "little sky" was well received and that you were not disappointed. I did indeed receive the photos but did not write sooner, as I thought you were away. Your portrait from behind is finished, and "le monde poétique" [*The Poetic World*] as well. They are just waiting to be thoroughly dry before being sent to you. I think you will very much like your portrait, which is called *Not to Be Reproduced* [*La Reproduction interdite*], and I am eager to know how it strikes you, and Dalí as well (I suppose he is in London for some time?). My next painting is a response to the theme of the dancer.... Since getting back here, I have painted *The Harsh Cure* [*La Guérison sévère*] or *The Pleasure Principle* [*Le Principe de plaisir*]—the figure whose head is replaced by a bright light—and *The Traveler* [*Le Voyageur*], which is the globe composed of objects (bust of a woman, stone, barrel, armchair, trumpet, etc.) I told you about.

And you, dear friend, have you been working some? I am sorry that I do not read English, because judging from the poem you wrote in French, I'm sure I would enjoy getting better acquainted with what you do.

I hope you derived great benefit from your rest cure and that you are in good health.

If, as I suppose, Dalí is in London, would you be good enough to give him my best regards? Thanks, dear friend, and best wishes.

Magritte

Jette-Brussels, May 6, 1938
135 Rue Esseghem

My dear James,

What happened? I haven't heard from you, yet I was sure you would have been to see my exhibition at the London Gallery. Nor have I heard from Mesens. I wrote to him several times. I'll end up believing that my letters to England are like messages in a bottle cast into the sea.

I hope there is some simple explanation for this alarming state of affairs.

Over the summer, a group of independent artists came up with the plan of mounting a big three-month exhibition at the Palais des Beaux-Arts in Brussels. The point is to provide a truly modern example of the museum and teach the "authorities" who officially preside over museums a lesson. I have been asked for some paintings for this exhibition.

Wouldn't that be a good opportunity for you to come over to Brussels? I would quite like to see you again. In due time, I'll send you details about the dates.

I have a "peacock" pigeon that left, and, in my garden this morning, a sparrow flew off when it saw me. I am thinking a lot about birds for the moment, and about a complete transformation of my painting.

I believe I am pushing on even further than I had up to now with an approach that seems very clear to me at present: when I didn't show an object in a painting … I justified the procedure by decreeing:

an object may be replaced by its image
an object may be replaced by its name
an object may be replaced by any form
an object may be replaced by any word.

This seemed to me to demonstrate what occurs in everyday life. In fact, we have words to designate what we do not see or know: our heart, death, etc.

But now that I have seen some of Penrose's collages in London, I am struck by something that happens in them which could result in unexpected developments: while ordinarily colors are used to represent objects, Penrose has succeeded in using images of objects to represent colors! Having thought a lot about it (and a text I am writing on the subject is soon to be published), it occurred to me that the procedures mentioned above could take on an entirely new meaning: these objects that I do not represent or that I sometimes represent in the shadow *have lost their colors*. And that is why they are evoked by something other than a brightly lit image of them.

I am at present working on a painting based on these points: *The Domain of Arnheim* [*Le Domaine d'Arnheim*], a tribute to Poe's tale, which in my opinion could lead to thoughts like this one: we move mountains so the sun will appear in accordance with a given desire.

If you come to Brussels this summer, you will see the results of this new experiment.

Do write, my dear James, and be assured of my best regards.

Magritte

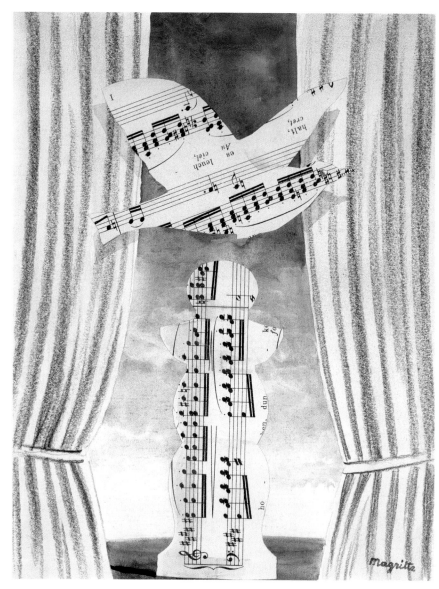

First Loves (*Les Premiers Amours*), 1961. Papier collé, gouache and crayon on paper, 25 x 19 cm. Private collection, courtesy Odermatt-Vedovi, Paris

Jette-Brussels, July 26, 1938
135 Rue Esseghem

My dear James,

I have the impression that you have suddenly lost interest in the role you have to play. It is not a question of a right or a compulsion, but of a fact: you, along with a few rare men of whom I am one, form a peculiar society. For us, money is only a means in current use, and nothing more. It so happens that by chance you have more of it than you need, and I, too little. It would be perfectly fitting and "above board" for you to provide me with some from time to time, as you had begun to do. For my part, I produce objects which are highly important, whatever stupid people in general may think.

To avoid all "commercial" considerations in the future, I propose the following ritual: you will send me £100 at the beginning of every August until 19.., and in exchange you will receive what I consider the best picture of those recently completed.

I am writing to you as I paint, with complete contempt for the ambiguous habits of "respectable" society, my only concern being *what ought to be*, the world such as it is, not yet having completely succeeded in wiping me out.

I hope you are in good health and that my "call to order" will find in you, precisely, its best justification.

With all friendly feelings, my dear James,

Magritte

English translation quoted from David Sylvester (ed.), *René Magritte. Catalogue Raisonné*, vol. 2, Houston: Menil Foundation/Antwerp: Fonds Mercator, 1993, pp. 61-2.

Monday, [August 1, 1938]

My dear James,

I am answering right away because I see that there are some slight errors in your feelings in regard to me. I ask you not to think of my previous letter as an unpleasantness any longer. I quite like you, and I believe the feeling is to a certain extent mutual. However, my friends are in the habit of requiring certain things of me, and that is the only way I conceive of friendship. Perhaps it is just a deception, like so many others. If it is a deception, I admit that I am easy prey, though at times it is quite painful.

Given this statement, let me explain myself: I am gratified that you start your letter by acknowledging my frankness. But I am sorry that you proceed immediately to make an ironical reference to my "charming naiveté." This irony is highly questionable.

Once again, I claim to take notice of a very few men, who appear to be commanded by a single demon. And they must not be confused with the countless artistic fabricators you may have encountered in your life.

You provide proof that you do indeed have at your disposal too much money for your needs—real needs, I mean—since part of this money is already earmarked for children who do not yet exist, for problematical beings. You also make money into something more than a means, since in your given situation you turn it into a pretext for worry! I hope for your sake that you can be amused by games other than that.

How, my dear James, can you contrast the fact of your tireless interest in all I do with your capacity to become a great writer? If that strikes you as incompatible, then your reasoning is incomprehensible to me. Either you have a superficial liking for what I do, which is quite possible, or else you deem the experiments and explorations I undertake to be of interest. I refuse to believe that that could be detrimental to your destiny. Please be aware that compliments and mockery are both entirely incapable of altering my concerns, and that in this particular realm of creation, the so-called self-confidence you attribute to me does not come into play.

I know very well that you truly like all those fine things you have collected, but my feelings about their possible future gold-currency value are clear and simple: if they are an object of speculation, then I hope they will always be a complete and utter disappointment to those who acquire them with a view to selling them at a huge profit later. That would help make it easier to suppress any art business.

Now, my dear James, that we have cleared up a few points, I express once more my regret at having written to you the way I did. I wrote my previous letter without perhaps making myself quite clear and should no doubt have realized that this was so indispensable. Your delightful suggestion makes me both happy and unhappy. I would very much like to see Italy. But many things still prevent me from undertaking the project: as I already mentioned, my wife's father is very sick, and, for the moment, were she to leave, she would have no peace of mind. When I can contemplate making this trip, I will set up a rendez-vous with you and be glad if you are still willing to have me at that time. In the meanwhile, dear friend, all the best to you from my wife and from

Magritte

English translation partly quoted from David Sylvester (ed.), *René Magritte. Catalogue Raisonné*, vol. 2, Houston: Menil Foundation/Antwerp: Fonds Mercator, 1993, pp. 62-3.

135 Rue Esseghem
Jette-Brussels
Friday, December 8, 1939

My dear friend,

I just received your letter of November 20 and am pleased to learn that the Marchioness of Casafuerte received what you wished me to send her.

As for the discrepancy caused by the drop in the pound, I reckon that your very kind gesture compensates for the difference.

I seem to understand that despite the bother you speak of (notaries, customs officials, etc.), you are in excellent moral health, and I hope that the same may be said of your physical health.

I have nothing to crow about in that regard. I often have pains in my chest and am continually dizzy. According to a doctor "of vessels," it seems that it is my nerves that are unwell. I ought to give up smoking, drinking alcohol (I hardly ever drink), making love, and all nervous fatigue. How does that sound to you?

As for my morale, I am not exactly troubled by the war: the air we breathe is still just as poisoned as before, and my lack of fitness for the sordid life, of which I feel the advantages and disadvantages, seems quite permanent. All in all, I do not hope for much from the future or the past.

Except for a few moments of compensation, there is little cause for joy.

I am delighted to see that you are ready to open the door at which the admirable fairy of the invisible has come knocking. You will recognize her, for you have all the gifts and know the courtesies required by the customs of this enchanted folk. I myself had a visit one night from an ambassador of that land of candle-lit salons. He was a curious personage composed of irregular plaques of nocturnal marble upon which the word "Bel Canto" was engraved in calligraphy, and he was very big and hid a large portion of a winter landscape, where above snow-covered roofs there was a very luminous blue sky ... To give this character a name, I think we have to say "The Midday Moon."

I will convey your greetings to Scutenaire, who will be touched. He is sorry not to have a constitution that would allow him to join the French Foreign Legion, for he really likes the spectacular side of the war and ill-tempered people. When he comes over to see me, he grabs some object to use as a rifle and bombards my friends and me, going "Pow! Pow!" in his husky lawyer voice, and then imitates cannon fire—воом! in a deep tone.

Do not fail to write, my dear friend, and see you soon perhaps? Best regards,

Magritte

The First Day (*Le Premier Jour*), [1943]. Crayon on paper, 29 x 22 cm.
Private collection

Bernard Noël

A Surrealist Outpost: The Magritte Society

For Magritte, thought, poetry and painting were not three different activities: they were three dimensions he combined in such a way that the third of them, ostensibly the only one he practiced, would interact with the other two and summon a fourth—call it "mystery"—to unfurl in the presence of a sensitive intelligence. The order I have listed these dimensions in is not arbitrary, for Magritte's primary concern was not painting, even though it is to painting that he owed his fame. Painting is, after all, a mental activity, and too bad for painters who misconstrue their terrain. The problem is that they must find their way out of painting by means of painting, or if you will, find their way out of representation by means of representation. This realization was a preliminary to Surrealist reasoning; however, conceiving an attitude is not the same as adhering to it. The temptation has always been greater to excel in appearance than to change one's own life from the inside.

Magritte was unwavering in his fidelity to this choice, because he very quickly grasped that it is impossible to change life without first changing the way one sees it, especially since this change alone might just suffice. Instead of acting the artist and playing at the avant-garde, he returned to Brussels, where he assumed the modest air of someone who might be his employee, with the full measure of self-mockery and normality this disparity implies. The surprising thing is that his position quickly became central to a friendly group consisting mostly of writers, all of whom had made up their minds not to pursue a career as a writer. Three became remarkable: Marcel Lecomte, Paul Nougé and Louis Scutenaire. A fourth, who was younger, joined them later: Marcel Mariën. But to name only these writers, for having left a body of work that was eventually recognized, would be unfair to the others: Colinet, Goemans, Mesens, Souris and Paul Magritte, the composer-cum-poet brother. Nor should the companions be forgotten: Georgette Magritte, Irène Hamoir and Marthe Nougé. These friends got together often, at cafés, at the Magrittes', at one or another of their homes. They formed an "anonymous" society, in that, unlike the Parisian groups, they preferred to go unnoticed and not to possess any power. The general spirit was close to Alfred Jarry and to Gérard de Nerval walking a lobster on a leash in the gardens of the Palais Royal. They liked jokes, irony and devastating turns of phrase, but all with a sense of gravity, that is, keeping their ears tuned to the echo that returned their remarks with an accent from beyond. Solidarity never served as springboard, and each of them used the prison of the human condition as a means of escape.

This society, "acephalic" well before the one imagined by Bataille and Masson, engaged in "collective invention" for which Magritte provided the material without assuming the role of chief or pope. A painting by Magritte was not finished until it received a title; this happened at a little ceremony—Mariën called it an "entitlement" (*intitulation*)—that seems to have formed the Society's fundamental bond.

This entitlement was both a game and a mental exercise. In addition, it served as a kind of test for those wishing to join the Society, a covert initiation rite. This operation provides a glimpse of the site of Magritte's work, which was pictorial in form and technique but treated the picture in a way no one ever had before. Here was a series of images, all identifiable at first glance yet all equally disturbing, because the object—albeit an ordinary object—has undergone a mutation of position, size or material that pushes our eye to its limit, makes it falter. Hence, some people burst out laughing at this zaniness; others make a readjustment, regulating the eye to a strange form of visualization that makes seeing and thinking inseparable.

The title ties the knot that binds sight and thought by reestablishing the natural interpenetration of the visual and the mental. Paul Nougé wrote, "The title of a painting, if it is effective, does not mold itself to the picture in the manner of a more or less subtle and appropriate commentary. But under the picture's guidance, the title springs forth from an illumination analogous to that which determined what it is the title puts a name to. The best titles arise in this way. Others, the ones that come through a purely logical and conscious search, betray themselves by this vague air of emptiness. They are deniable at will."

Finding the right title demonstrated one's capacity to achieve a state of receptivity to the painting so true that perceiving the painting precipitated its perfect verbal expression. The title corresponds to what the painting makes visible. It is the fruit born of the instantaneous passage from illumination to expression. Scutenaire, who took part in entitlement sessions from 1926 until Magritte's death, fondly remembered the way titles bounced from one participant to another and the aura of overpowering obviousness that surrounded the sudden appearance of the right one. As he described the moment, it seems that a transmutation occurred between the visual and the verbal and remained embedded in the painting, waiting for the viewer who could reactivate it.

The Society published many tracts, reviews, booklets and postcards illustrated by Magritte, who detested holding on to his paintings and far preferred them as reproductions. These activities attest to "collective invention." However, if all the participants wrote about Magritte's painting, only two did so in any substantial way: Paul Nougé and Louis Scutenaire.

The importance of their work leaves no room for doubt; however, it might do well to inject a note of reservation, because time and death have altered the available perspective: what Nougé and Scutenaire left scattered in their lifetimes has been gathered up in book form. Today, Nougé's *Magritte à travers tout le reste* is an important part of his collected works, but the writings it is made up of were published separately between 1933 and 1948. To Magritte, Nougé's reflections were proof of the excellence of his method: thus, they played a discrete but considerable role. Nougé was more attentive to thought than to the wielding of the brush, more sensitive to ethics than to plastic values. But, as much a poet as a thinker, he knew what inhabited the painted object when it acquired the emotive power of a being. Magritte had faith in both Nougé's intellectual breadth and his ability to fix a mystery the way one prepares a chemical precipitate whose process remains invisible. The invisible remains secret, but its presence is sufficient. Despite their similarity, or perhaps because of it, Magritte and Nougé quarreled on various occasions, and their rupture of September 1952 was final.

After Nougé's death in 1967, Scutenaire bought the portrait Magritte had painted of him in 1927. "Scut" lived in Brussels, on Rue de la Luzerne, with fifty of Magritte's paintings, each representative of a key moment in his oeuvre. He asserted his Picard identity and considered his street Picardy's northernmost border. But introducing this incidental fact only serves to delay an unpleasant memory. One day, when I went to visit him alone, and not as usual with one or more friends from Brussels, Scut took me upstairs to a cold, dark room and suddenly stood me in front of Nougé's portrait. He pointed out some marks in the lower part of the painting that, too struck by the whole, I had not seen: cigarette burns.

These burn marks scandalized Scut, who saw them as vandalism on Nougé's part: a deliberate sabotaging of the old friendship. To me, they revealed the scars of a friendship that no doubt had received its share through ruptures and death, so that the only thing the members of the dissolved Society had left was a painful corpse lying in state amid fond memories. That was 1977, the year Scutenaire saw the publication of *Avec Magritte*, which brought together in one volume everything he had written about his friend between 1942 and 1976. Although the project was not his idea, he had agreed to it.

Scutenaire's book is as essential as Nougé's, but from the opposite standpoint. Nougé deals with the oeuvre, its conceptual process and meaning; Scutenaire deals with the man—his ways, relationships, everyday activities, habits—from all of which he bit by bit erects the strong presence of a personality as original in his behavior as in his art. The book is laid out in fragments: some are very short; others run to two pages. These fragments are a mixture of anecdotes, glimpses and brief, instantaneous reflections. Some examples: "Magritte is a great painter, Magritte is not a painter." —"Magritte is a practical joker according to the critics. It's true, Magritte is also a practical joker."—"He would rather give than receive, even money."—"He holds the same opinions as everybody else on matters where you would expect him to be an individualist and has unusual ideas on subjects about which you would not expect him to have any opinion at all."—"Seen from the outside, his life is that of a bourgeois with a love of the baroque, a touch of madness and a taste for false situations."

These few examples furthermore paint a counter-portrait of Scutenaire and his predilection for the revelatory power of a delicate balance. Magritte never had a studio: he didn't take himself for a painter. Yet he exhibited, sold and earned a living from his painting. His friends greatly helped him to be the creator of paintings that sold, without being an artist who made a career of it. On the other hand, Scutenaire and Nougé were writers without being so through the Society's publications, which remained confidential. One made his living from science, the other from the law; but their writing was recognized by their peers even in Paris. They formed a Surrealist outpost that turned a critical eye towards Surrealism, which struck them as quite professional and worldly. Although they shared its space, they held to their invisibility—all the more freely since their friend Magritte made things visible on behalf of all.

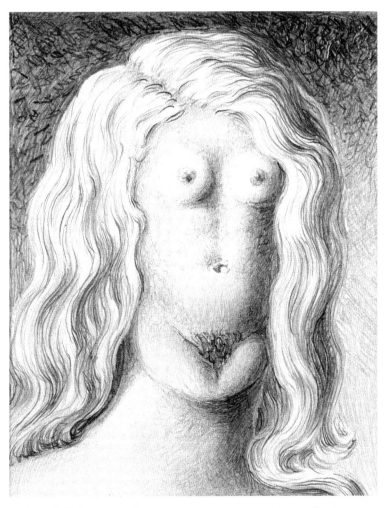

The Rape (*Le Viol*), ca. 1959. Crayon on paper, 14 x 11 cm. Private collection

My dear philosopher, yes, philosopher, for do you know, despite your knowledge and wisdom, why Churchill is such a favorite with the young? Because he said it would be long and hard and that he would see it through to the end—it seems that a little boy got a good laugh out of the story, so his parents apprehensively asked him what he thought it meant. He answered that he immediately understood it was about taking a crap.

After this preamble, due to my courtesy, let's move on to serious matters: there aren't any. Will we have the pleasure of seeing you Sunday? Of course, you would have to be mad to venture out in this heat and risk falling victim to the cold. But with your strong build, that is approximately the right word for it, I do not doubt whether you would hesitate to make a very necessary though very superfluous journey. And finally, but this is not the last of it, I advise you that for the moment I am a bit short and contemplate the future with anxiety, I would need a fairly substantial steady income, without having to worry about its prompt disbursal. Could you not in your kindness provide me an easy means of satisfying this desire? Thank you for your card, written in a suitable style, and many things to the both of you.

Magritte

My dear member,

Having failed to inquire of you in the heat of the discussion Sunday whether you would be dropping by next Sunday, without prejudice to the eventuality of potatoes and onions, in order that we might know if we should await confirmation of your visit, I ask you, if it is not too great an imposition upon your kindness, to let us know by telephone or post of your intentions for next Sunday, so that if you are not to be our guest, we might either go to the movies or ourselves accept an invitation to be the guests of some kind host, although we do not as yet quite know what we would opt for on that day of rest, should you decide to go to Ollignies to visit your grandmother, who at the present time must be thrilled at the prospect of probably having you as a guest next Sunday, and I am delighted on her behalf, although I should have preferred that you be our guests, but then, your grandmother being deprived of the pleasure, I would, instead of being pleased about her pleasure had you gone to see her, I would, I say, share her disappointment, but my pleasure would be greater than my compassion for her, which would not be too great, for I think the people of Ollignies are easily consoled if visitors chance to leave them in the lurch, given their discretion, which you did not fail to ingest with your mother's milk, which likewise allowed you to grow in the shadow of the threatening table and gave you a love of animals and friendly feelings toward hosts who, like me, share pleasing aromas with you. See you soon. M…

[1943]

My dear Scut,

For the book in preparation, we could use a color reproduction of *Panic in the Middle Ages* [*La Panique au Moyen Âge*]. Only I would have to have the painting (without the frame) Monday morning at the latest. If your reluctance to transport a work of art to my house on Sunday at the time of your probable visit is less pronounced than the enthusiasm you would feel in thinking about the honors of making a color snapshot, would you please wrap the painting in paper and escort it to my house? Ask Irène at any rate. For the rest, I do not delude myself, the case is already lost; for my part I am reconciled to it, it is a matter of dragging a rather drab existence out to the end. Bookkeeping does more harm than good.
See you soon, and a good butt fuck to Irène,

M.

[1947]

Mr. M…,

So there is perhaps a still-embryonic idea that you could shape and formulate.
All in "all," I have always represented things, matters, objects, people and animals with *clarity* [*netteté*],*
even if those things and matters were mysterious. Between that and desiring to enlighten even more brilliantly, there has been no unfortunate decision on my part, it seems to me. All the more so in that this enlightenment is the same as that of the Sun—a comrade not to be scorned lightly. This embryonic idea is given as a little jolt that might perhaps rock your balls.

   As for the question of genius, I trust you on that score, I believe you are capable of coming up with good final formulas. Along the lines of the variant of the celebrated *partir c'est mourir un peu* [to leave is to die a little], which I cannot recall without pride.

   For your guidance, here is a small gouache also in an embryonic state, which I don't feel like continuing with, but which still might serve as a frontispiece?

As I wait to hear from you, please accept, dear bugger, my friendly wishes with Irène.

M.

* Very important, I think: with *clarity*, but that does not mean that the images obtained are dull and devoid of mystery. On the contrary, while in paintings intended to convey a great "spiritual loftiness" and to speak to the soul, through an artistic "manner"—(these paintings do not even speak to the asshole), in my "clear" and "sunlit" painting, the enigma remains intact and dumbfounds the herd.

Dear muses,

It is a good idea, to slap paint onto the frames—and also the school riddled with cracks and the vermilion fellow. I also thought of a hat with an electric lamp. All that (like the cracked school, stamped with the mark of good taste) makes one a bit giddy. Anyway, I'm a bit giddy, perhaps it is due to that and to my sudden repose; I made the shipment for New York! Send ideas, as many as possible. You will have sketches until something better becomes available. The ad copy is quite good, even too good I fear—for this world is not made for good things.

Just the same, we will try once again (although I refrain from illusions: illusion is not a necessary or essential activity).

So, I am waiting for new ideas, work wonders, and meanwhile I'll see you a week from Saturday. Bugger yourselves for me.

M. the 1st

Dear monographists,

One thing to point out perhaps (it is reading Goemans's note that is to appear in *Les Beaux-Arts* next week that makes me think of it) is that people misuse the word "dream" in regard to my painting. We are perfectly willing to accept the dream realm's respectability—but my work is not oneiric, *quite the contrary*.

    If it deals with the "dream," it is a very different "dream" from the kind you have when you're asleep. On the contrary, it deals with very *willful* "dreams" that have nothing vague like the feelings you would have while lost in dreaming. And the will that makes me search for images that pass for dream images in the view of some is the will that a few of us have. It consists above all in making *the most light possible*. (Goemans says apropos of that: dreams that are made not to put us to sleep but to wake us up [or make us more alert].)

    Got a small parcel from Iolas (15,000), things could be worse! Ha! Ha! Got a nice letter from Fanny. I'll tell you about it at our next conclave.

Send good news of yourselves. Your friend,

Mag

Untitled, 1926. Papier collé, watercolor and crayon on paper, 50 x 40 cm.
Private collection

[Paris, 1948]

Dear compatriots,

In the foreign city I receive your card just at the moment I begin this letter. Here is the news all in a jumble: Exhibition opening with visitors, although with some Belgians: Lambrix who does not like the preface, something about the lack of thought he said, Servranckx drenched in rain because it began pouring buckets, Wergifosse who is assisting me. Many visitors from Paris and America. Hugnet whom I take for Brunius and from whom I ask news of Mesens to his great bewilderment and irritation. Jean-Marie to whom I say a firm and resounding "How do, Massa." A young American who is the living portrait of *The Psychologist* [*Le Psychologue*] and who has seen gangsters, dead and alive, in New York. This psychologist works for television and is going to film my exhibition Friday for an American television company. A Swiss woman, the wife of the gallery's boss, also does television, I said I would very much like to perform with her and it's the truth. For because of the ambiance and its psychological or Freudian effects, I have suitable and regular erections here. It would be interesting to see if that were to persist if I lived here all the time? Also saw Roux, whom I still confuse with Brun. We have spoken about you folks and fairly little else, not being particularly talkative. Anyway, after the opening, Labisse had prepared a cocktail party where there were thirty participants, among the best known were Queneau, J. L. Barrault and P. Brasseur. There was also someone from the Comédie Française (there is lots of ass at the Comédie Française and it is a delight). The sad mechanism of the human spirit was manifest, as I might have expected: Barrault, who was speaking to me, was soon eclipsed by Brasseur, who also wanted to be prominent. So I promptly started saying "tu" to him, like a little boy, and with the fumes from the cocktails egging me on, I said to his wife: I am going to plop a little more whisky in your mix.

Labisse has a mill at Knokke-le-Zoute where it is possible to spend vacations. Here, he has a studio with his wife, who is a tall spindle of a thing with blond hair. His apartment is above his studio, the bathroom is above the W.C. There are lots of pictures and cards and magazines with crimes in color and mannequins like the ones in department stores.

Anyway, it doesn't make you giddy. I much like the idea of circulating strong boxes, commodes, coffins, etc. I hope to hear from you again because it is a great spiritual comfort.

I am sending a catalogue to Wolf.

Friendly greetings,

Mag

P.S. Märien asked me to write to him but at the moment I have a hangover and would rather you give him the news on my behalf. Thanks in advance, and that way you'll have the advantage of a fruitful contact with Märien.

Dear Irène and Scut,

This is no doubt the last holograph ejaculation I will offer you from Paris. In taking our bearings, we come up with a sum of zero, as our acquaintances had us anticipate. (Zero if the results are measurable.) Spiritually, however, I made a few acquisitions: I think for example (temporarily) that what distinguishes us from the thinking [of geniuses?] (despite ourselves, because wanting to distinguish oneself at all cost is out of the question), is our total lack of belief in form and content. The very active here seem to latch onto form, the only bone left for them to gnaw on. Such as that rotten Baron Molet, who was sweetness and light with me and tells it all around that "*les pieds dans le plat*" ("putting one's foot in it") will not do in Paris (it is true that it will not do, but not in the way that imbecile understands it). Content: feelings are "at heart" perfectly indifferent, "'cept" when you feel them in everyday life (outside literature).

All this leads me to think that my "business" of a painting enterprise boils down to simple manufacturing, like making old furniture. Surrounding this enterprise, there are other forms of craft, like those of the writer, the theatrical crowd and … and all this constitutes the World of the Arts—the forms and content of which, however, mean nothing to me.

At the exhibition, there are visitors (young women have a tendency to laugh, but they hold back, since it is not proper in art galleries). Visitors spouting the usual crock "it's not so profound as before," it's "Belgian wit," "one senses that it is not Parisian," what a brushstroke! what a fine torso (for *The Psychologist* [*Le Psychologue*]), etc. There was a review in *Arts*, which you can obtain in Brussels. Unable to buy you a copy and send it. I feel nauseated just thinking about it. Sales, too, stand at zero up to now; that may change, nothing is definitely spoken for. "Sooo" for pleasure, we mostly go for walks in the Bois de Vincennes, which is close by our digs, and that way we don't have to put up with traveling about and noise. For pleasure there are good delicatessens here. I am waiting for an announced visit from Iolas—in a day or two—even if he doesn't come or is late, I'm clearing out Thursday. If you like, we could get together Friday at my place as usual. Got a letter from Fanny with accounts. I will show it to Irène, as I am not up to it myself.

Hope to see you soon, and hearty erections,

M.

The Red Model (*Le Modèle rouge*), 1947 or 1948. Gouache on paper, 48 x 37 cm.
Private collection, Switzerland

Daniel Abadie

René Magritte and Alexander Iolas: The Art of Conversation

Since the birth of modern painting, the artist and the dealer have formed an inseparable yet seemingly impossible couple, so opposed do their interests at first appear. Nor is this odd match immune to the classic vicissitudes of saturation, jealousy, infidelity and arguments over money, which eventually spawn a deep attachment, strengthened by trials and tribulations. Of Magritte's various dealers, from the Galerie du Centaure to Camille Goemans, from E. L. T. Mesens to Lou Cosyn, only Alexander Iolas was able to keep the relationship going for more than twenty years, from 1946 until Magritte's death in 1967. This is all the more surprising in that their contact seemed the most improbable, the least likely to last, each seeing the other as a mate from hell. What could be farther removed from Magritte's calculated contentment with a middle-class Belgian façade (dark overcoat, bowler hat) and his accountant-style letters, recriminating over a few days' delay in remittance, than the whimsy and nonchalant lightheartedness of the ex-dancer Iolas (he had been with the Monte Carlo ballet company), who deliberately ignored the rules of both society and the banks?

Except for two and a half years spent at Le Perreux, on the outskirts of Paris, in 1927–30, Magritte left Brussels (where his parents had settled in 1917), his wife Georgette and his succession of Pomeranians only briefly and without enjoyment. In addition, his cultural focus was so thoroughly French that, despite his success in the United States, he never learned any more English than André Breton. In view of the painter's home-loving and insular attitude, the Egyptian-born Greek immigrant to the United States, Alexander Iolas—a remarkable polyglot with a showy character and ready repartees abetted by a provocative sense of humor who simultaneously owned galleries in Paris, New York, Geneva, Milan and Madrid in the 1960s—would no doubt have been an insufferable phenomenon to Magritte. That is, if the latter had not, under his anonymous, polished bourgeois mask, conserved a deep-seated rebelliousness and rejection of social norms, which came out in forms all the more excessive for being short-lived—the "Vache" period in his painting; the deliberate vulgarity of his letters to Scutenaire; his membership, in right-minded royalist Belgium, in the Communist Party.

Otherwise unconcerned with keeping records, Alexander Iolas nonetheless saved the entirety of his correspondence with Magritte, through moves and changes of country and continent. In January 1979, he donated it to the Menil Foundation through his intermediary André Mourgues. This impressive body of 314 letters (192 of them written by Magritte) enables us to follow the ups and downs of the artist–dealer relationship from 1946 until just before Magritte's death and see how, over the years, a true partnership and friendship developed between the two.

Magritte first made direct contact with Iolas, without realizing it, in a letter of reply dated February 27, 1946, in which he agrees to an exhibition of his works at the Hugo Gallery, New York, in December 1946. At first thinking Iolas was simply an employee of the gallery, he addressed his letter to Maria Hugo, the gallery's titular owner, whom he did not know either. However, Hugo, the widowed Duchesse de Gramont and very well connected in New York society, contributed only her name and address book to the gallery. Iolas's proposal of a solo exhibition was all the more appealing to the painter in that two previous New York shows (at the Julien Levy Gallery in 1936 and 1938) had been unsuccessful both in sales and in achieving recognition. So it is not surprising that in April 1946, Magritte was worrying about gallery visitors' reaction to the paintings he had consigned through F. Lee: "I would be most grateful, too," he wrote, "to be apprised of the public's response to my painting and of any information you might care to give me on this subject."

Thus began a long period during which Magritte complained of Iolas's inexactness, the announced visits that never materialized and the letters left unanswered. On November 13, 1946, he wrote to Maria Hugo, "I expected a visit from your director, who was in Europe this summer, to discuss the details of an

Magritte, Alexander Iolas and William Lieberman, Museum of Modern Art, New York, 1965

exhibition at the Hugo Gallery. What has become of the plans we spoke about?" The gallery finally presented works by Magritte in spring 1947, from April 7 to 30. Acting as project manager for the undertaking, Magritte included several of his recent "Renoir" period paintings, which failed to satisfy the taste of New York art lovers and especially Iolas, who returned *The Harvest* (*La Moisson*), *A Stroke of Luck* (*La Bonne Fortune*), *The Smile* (*Le Sourire*), *Black Magic* (*La Magie noire*) and *The Daughter of the Great Secret* (*La Fille du grand secret*) to the painter.

It was not until fall 1947 that Magritte finally met Iolas, to whom he wrote on November 12,

"I was waiting to hear from you as you promised when you were here in Brussels, and I am happy to learn that you have returned safely to New York and that your intentions regarding our exhibition projects remain favorable. For my part, I haven't lost sight of the goal to be reached, and I believe I can state that in due course you will receive a group of pictures of prime importance. I also believe that the role played by chance will be reduced to a minimum, for previous experience and your information enable me to adjust my aim. I do not mean to say that it is simple—in my case— for it is impossible for me to take only a 'commercial' interest. On the contrary, my essential preoccupation has not been abandoned: it is still true poetic density, the search for a certain mental substance that is necessary to man living in these times."

Iolas's reply of November 21 confirms that they shared the same point of view:

"I agree with you that what is required is poetic painting, and of very fine quality. That alone will sell, and that alone is what I have asked you for. The people who like your painting prior to 1940 do so because they unanimously find it more poetic and superior to those five paintings I returned to you, and these people are very inclined towards owning the old ones. Believe me as a friend and great admirer that what I want above all is to ensure that your work receives the recognition that is its immediate due. No, you need not concern yourself with the business end of things, I will take care of that for you the instant I have paintings the equal of *The Red Model* [*Le Modèle rouge*], *The Future* [*L'Avenir*] and others like them. Nor do I ask you to copy these older paintings, just not to interrupt the poetic and mysterious quality of your old paintings, which in their concise technique were much more Magritte than those where the Renoiresque brushwork and coloring strike everyone as outmoded."

If Magritte did not conceal a certain disappointment at the reception of his work in New York,[1] he was nevertheless careful, while preserving his artist's pride, to appease his dealer, to whom he wrote on November 27,

"The painting that you call 'Renoiresque' is over and done with, and the pictures from this period will be much sought after 'later.' But this experience will have helped me develop many points, and as a result, among other things, you will be able to compare the new works with the older ones, such as *The Red Model*, entirely to the advantage of the new ones."

In Magritte and Iolas's case, no doubt owing to the artist's precarious financial situation, it is the painter who was preoccupied with accounting and the dealer who was more concerned with the image of his artist—

1 On April 21, 1947, Magritte wrote to Iolas apropos of Tyler's preface for the catalogue: "I find it very sympathetic, although I do not for an instant agree with the meaning he gives my paintings when he says they are 'charades.' Such a commonplace interpretation surprises me, coming from a contributor to *View*, just like his comments on the titles: there is nothing gratuitous or arbitrary about a title like *The Smile* (*Le Sourire*), for example. What the painting evokes brings a peculiar smile to the viewer's lips, which justifies the title."

the inverse of the usual painter–dealer relationship, where the dealer looks primarily after business matters and the painter takes care of the art. In a letter of January 18, 1950, that begins "My love and dear Mr. Magritte," Iolas deals quickly with the painter's request for payment before continuing matter-of-factly,

"Now let's move on to much more serious topics than money. I am very intrigued by the four paintings, but I beg you first to send sketches, for this time we can no longer allow ourselves the luxury of presenting to the American public paintings that do not represent you and that are not masterpieces. These four paintings must be painted divinely and with all your poetry and genius. I like the bottles very much, but I make no secret of the fact that I am disappointed by the gouaches, they are satyrical and to a certain extent resemble in spirit the gouaches from the Paris exhibition,[2] which would be a disaster here…. Do not think ill of me if I try and enlighten you about the American public, but you must succeed in making your name with the

upcoming exhibition, it must be sublime and astonishing. And I am more than certain you will accomplish this miracle, for a miracle is needed."

Magritte's down-to-earth answer—"As usual, I do not know what to think of our affairs, is the Hugo Gallery still in existence?"[3]—did not prevent him from perceiving in time that, beyond the late payments and vague accounting, he had in Iolas a true advocate and admirer of his work. "I am happy to know that the interest you show in me resists the passage of time. For my part, I greatly appreciate the qualities you reveal and the way you defend my work," he wrote to Iolas on January 16, 1958.

The correspondence with Iolas also gave the painter the chance to send out feelers, to test his new and sometimes eccentric ideas. On March 29, 1956, he suggested, "Certain pictures like *The Place in the Sun* [*La Place au soleil*][4] could be done over; for a woman's portrait, the face would replace that of the *Primavera*. Or for a man, the face would replace that of the *Scribe*, and so on. All I would need is a good photograph of the lady or gentleman, with indications of hair and eye color, and so on."

Perhaps that is why the last of these letters, dated December 28, 1966, announces that Magritte is sending Iolas a new painting entitled *The Idea* (*L'Idée*).

---

2 At the Galerie du Faubourg in 1948.
3 Magritte, letter to Iolas, February 28, 1950.
4 Former title of *The Ready-made Bouquet* (*Le Bouquet tout fait*).

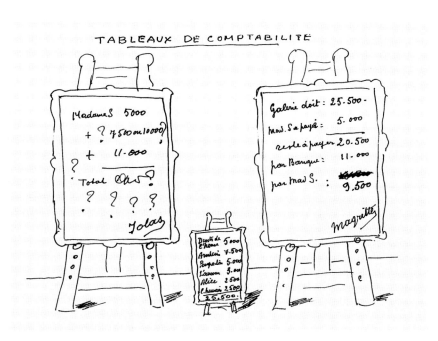

Drawing by Magritte accompanying his complaints about the irregular payments by Iolas's Hugo Gallery. Private collection

Jette-Brussels
2-28-1950
135 Rue Esseghem

Mr. Iolas
Hugo Gallery, New York

Dear friend,

As usual, I do not know what to think of our affairs, is the Hugo Gallery still in existence?

I am working in very unfavorable conditions: I just finished a new picture (a new idea I had) that I am certain of, but is there any point in sending it to you? According to the newspapers here, these days America is an anxious nation, where the idea of war is very much on everyone's mind. I don't know whether the buyers of paintings in your milieu might have lost interest in art? You have not given me any precise or useful information.

What am I to think? I had hoped that through your co-operation, I might be able to work in relative peace, that purchases of paintings at prices advantageous to you would make things easier, but I find that I am, as always, faced with a lack of regularity in the gallery's payments to me and fear I am to learn that it has ceased operation?

I appeal to your personal interest in my works and ask you to be kind enough to understand my situation and do all you can in order that my activity should ensure you the greatest enjoyment. If I must reserve the latest paintings and gouaches for you, I must refuse to sell them here and not try and sell them. In that case, the Hugo Gallery's purchases would have to be settled regularly, and this is not what happens—payments are not only late, but incomplete and sporadic.

I remind you that you were thinking of having an exhibition in April. Is this project still on? Can I let myself believe that, if you do the exhibition, you will do it with conviction? That you will employ the proper means to give it the best chances: catalogue (with the reproductions and text I sent you), illustrations in magazines, and so on? Or else, if current living conditions in America do not make such an exhibition desirable, what *exactly* do you contemplate?

Could you also see that, in the future, the gallery's purchases are paid for promptly?

In this regard, I am still waiting for payment of 9,500 francs in arrears (4,500 for the gallery and 5,000 for your accountant).

Mme Sasonof long ago paid me the 10,000 francs you gave her sister. In the future, she is willing to give me the amounts you have her sister hold. But this method is uncertain. Surely you have some faster and more direct means available to you for making payment?

I hope to hear from you soon, for if you are doing the exhibition in April, I will have to see about the permits and prepare my works for shipping to the gallery.

Very cordially yours,

Magritte

P.S. In your letter of the 9th of this month, you ask the title of the painting illustrated in an American magazine. It is called *Perpetual Motion* [*Le Mouvement perpétuel*]. I may perhaps make a variant of this painting. I had written to you just before receiving that letter.

My dear Iolas,

I have your letter of February 25. In the meantime, I wrote to you on February 26.

I am sorry, but I am at a complete loss to understand your letter, and in order to get results, I ask that you clarify the following, point by point:

1) Your judgments of my works, do they depend on the works' ability to attract a buyer?

I ask you this because, until now, you have advised me not to send paintings with roses, and now you are asking for one because a lady likes roses?

I would like to point out that I can take this attitude into consideration, but in that case it is merely a matter of business and not an artistic judgment of my works. I have done paintings *against* the taste of those who buy paintings: for example, *The Red Model, [Le Modèle rouge*], and the idea of doing such a painting with old shoes, was not about to, and did not, appeal to buyers when it was *new*. At present, with time, buyers have come to like this painting (you have sold quite a few replicas), but that is no reason to believe buyers are more intelligent now than they were fifteen years ago, when *no one* would buy the first *Red Model*.

Obviously, I bear this factor in mind in this sense: it is useless to send *only* new paintings to America. Some are necessary because there is a slight chance they will find purchasers. What is especially needed is replicas of known and accepted paintings. I enclose a photo of a painting with roses. It measures 73 x 50 cm. I can send it to you if you like. If this is a firm purchase, let me know by return mail, and you can have it for 6,000 francs. If you take it on deposit, I will count it as 9,000 francs. I await your decision in this matter.

2) You can't return the gouaches and paintings you haven't sold, because they left for America as "sold." Could you bring them back to me yourself when you come to Europe? In that regard, I consider that paintings like *The Fall of the House of Usher* [*La Chute de la maison Usher*] and *The Assignation* [*Le Rendez-vous*], gouaches like *Blood Will Tell* (no. 3) [*La Voix du sang* (n° 3)] and *The Inner Gaze* [*Le Regard intérieur*] or *The Domain of Arnheim* (no. 2) [*Le Domaine d'Arnheim* (n° 2)] should not be destroyed just because no one bought them. Pardon me if I am unable to treat these matters blindly.

3) I am at a loss to understand the "accounting" issue you raise in a pleasant but confused manner. Enclosed is a clear reckoning that I ask you to pay as soon as possible: my dear friend, if you wish to avoid useless and tedious complications in our correspondence, I ask you to be kind enough to answer clearly each one of the above points and also the points in my letter of February 28.

You are in the business of selling paintings, and I make my living from my work. We have both chosen our occupations. Like you, I wish to sell a great deal. But not just anything.

It is evident that I could earn a lot of money by doing a certain type of painting for rich people with no taste, and you could earn more as well by selling this sort of monstrosity. We must come to terms with it—strike a balance between business and art! But in order to obtain the best results, let us not confuse art and business. So tell me with the *maximum* of *precision* what of my work has the best chance of being bought, which does not mean that what has not been sold (for example, the *sublime* gouache *The Cut-Glass Bath* [*Le Bain de cristal*]) must be torn up. This way, there will be no misunderstanding that might injure our business relationship or our feelings of what is fair.

I hope that from now on you will see fit to write your letters in two sections: a friendly section, which I am very eager for, where you tell me about your *personal taste*, and another, *very clear*, where you advise me about the painting market and matters pertaining to it.

I am keen to have your answers to all my questions, so that I will know where we stand.

With best wishes,
Magritte

Jette-Brussels, April 7, 1951
135 Rue Esseghem

Mr. Iolas
Hugo Gallery, New York

Dear friend,

I wrote you yesterday, and today I got your letter announcing that I will receive payment for the latest paintings you bought from me. I assume you mean that the necessary arrangements having been taken care of, and I will receive the sum of 25,000 francs in two or three days, around April 10 at the latest? I hope so, for that way I will no longer have to think of insisting upon greater regularity in our affairs. Furthermore, during your last visit to Brussels, you promised me an improvement in the resources I obtain from the Hugo Gallery, and I hope that this will still be possible?

I would have been happy to receive so much as a catalogue of my exhibition because I am keenly interested in it. I am waiting for the shipment of catalogues you also announced in your last letter.

As to the critics' reaction, it is to be expected. One need only realize once and for all how consistently the critics have been wrong so as not to be surprised at the routine reception of my latest works. As for my paintings, among the older ones such as *The Red Model* [*Le Modèle rouge*], *Black Magic* [*La Magie noire*] and so forth—which are at present more or less "recognized" due to their age—when they were younger and at the time when they were new, they met with this inevitable lack of comprehension from the newspaper critics. Therefore, in so far as I can fulfill your request for novelty, we are exposing ourselves to appearing shocking in the eyes of the journalists—whose opinion is as ephemeral as yesterday's news. Fortunately, from a practical standpoint, some people who buy paintings respond to something other than "the burning question of the moment."

I continue to work as in the past, without worrying over a certain public's frivolity. This is the time-tested way of achieving the best results. I finished *David's Madame Récamier* [*Mme. Récamier de David*] and am working on paintings that I will send you sketches or photos of. I hope to hear from you soon. Very cordially yours,

Magritte

Jette-Brussels, May 16, 1951
135 Rue Esseghem

Mr. Iolas
Hugo Gallery, New York

Dear friend,

What am I to make of your persistent silence?

I hope you are not ill or too busy to be able to write a note, and that I may attribute your silence to less serious reasons.

All the same, I would like to stay in touch and hear from you. Are you planning to come to Europe and stop by Brussels? In that case, I will have some sensational new paintings to show you.

I began a small picture, called *The Magician*, in which the person represented could have your features, making the painting a portrait at the same time. To do this, I must have *fairly quickly* three photos of you, taken by one of your friends with an easily obtainable, ordinary camera. I am enclosing instructions about how to proceed.

At any rate, I eagerly await word from you. Best regards,

Magritte

Magritte on a ladder in front of his mural *The Enchanted Domain* (*Le Domaine enchanté*),
at the Casino Communal, Knokke-le-Zoute, 1953

Sarah Whitfield

Chronology

1898

René-François-Ghislain Magritte was born on November 21 at 10 Rue de la Station, Lessines, the first child of Léopold and Régina Magritte.

1900

The family moved in May to 185 Chaussée de Fleurus, Gilly, where Magritte's brothers were born: Raymond-Firmin-Ghislain Magritte on June 29, 1900 (d. December 30, 1970, in Wemmel) and Paul-Alphonse-Ghislain Magritte on October 24, 1902 (d. October 15, 1975, in Blankenberge).

1904

The family moved in April to 77 Rue des Gravelles, Châtelet. The previous occupant of the house had been Régina's brother, who had used the ground floor as a butcher's shop. Léopold Magritte worked in the edible oil trade.

1905

In the autumn Magritte matriculated at the Ecole Moyenne in Châtelet.

1910

Magritte attended a weekly painting class given by a schoolmaster from the nearby town of Dampremy. Presumably it was at these classes, which took place in two rooms above a sweetshop, that he received his first lessons in oil painting. There are three extant oils from this year.

1911

In the course of the year, the family moved to a larger house at 95 Rue des Gravelles which was built specifically for them.

On the occasion of the Exposition de Charleroi, an international exhibition of arts and industry in the nearby town, which ran from the end of April to the end of November, a painting by Magritte of horses fleeing from a burning stable was displayed to the public in the hallway of the family house.

In November Magritte entered the Athenée Royal Mixte at Charleroi.

1912

In the early hours of February 24, Régina Magritte drowned herself in the Sambre after several previous suicide attempts; her body was not recovered until March 12. She was given a Christian burial.

1913

The household moved in March to 41 Rue du Fort, Charleroi.

In the spring or summer Magritte met his future wife, Georgette-Marie-Florence Berger (1901–86) at a fair in Charleroi.

1914

The Germans crossed the Belgian frontier on August 4, occupied Brussels on August 20 and were in control of all but a small corner of the country by October.

In October or November the family returned to their house in Châtelet.

1915

In November Magritte moved to Brussels and found accommodation in a boarding house at 122a Rue du Midi.

1916

In July–August Magritte showed four works in an arts and crafts exhibition in Châtelet. Two of these were drawings, a flayed horse and a wounded lioness; the other two were oil paintings, a still life and a landscape.

In October Magritte entered the Académie Royale des Beaux-Arts in Brussels, where he attended classes intermittently over the next five years. His teachers were Emile Vandamme-Sylva, Gisbert Combaz and

Portrait of Georgette Magritte, 1936. Drawing. Private collection

Constant Montald. He also attended classes on literature given by Georges Eekhoud, the novelist.

Magritte's family moved to Brussels in December and he resumed living with them. They stayed briefly at 21 Place Rouppe, a large house frequented by artists and teachers and students from abroad, where Magritte had been living since October. Afterwards they moved to 3 Rue des Foulons which, like the Place Rouppe, was a few minutes' walk from the Academy.

1917

In April the family, including Magritte, went back to Châtelet. They returned to Brussels in the autumn, moving into 43 Rue François-Joseph Navez, Schaerbeek, a large house with premises at the back for Léopold Magritte's new business, the manufacture of stock cubes.

1918

Magritte's earliest extant poster, advertising Pot au Feu Derbaix, was published in the course of this year.

1919

The first issue of the review *Au volant*, edited by Victor and Pierre Bourgeois and including Magritte on its editorial board, was published in April; the three remaining issues came out in the course of the year. Drawings by Magritte appeared in every number.

During the second half of 1919 and the first half of 1920 Magritte shared Pierre Flouquet's studio in the Rue des Alexiens.

In December Victor Bourgeois and Aimé Declercq opened the short-lived Centre d'Art in Brussels at 6 Rue Coudenberg. Magritte was represented in the inaugural exhibition in a section devoted to poster design.

1920

In January Magritte and Flouquet had a joint exhibition of paintings and poster designs at the Centre d'Art, Brussels.

At the time of the exhibition at the Centre d'Art, Magritte met Georgette Berger again in Brussels, where she had lately come to live and where she and her elder sister, Léontine, had found jobs at the Co-opérative Artistique.

The same month, Magritte met E. L. T. Mesens (1903-71), a young musician who

shared his enthusiasm for the avant-garde. Shortly afterwards they made contact with the Italian Futurists. Later they turned to Dada activity, encouraged by figures such as Erik Satie and Tristan Tzara, both of whom Mesens met in 1921.

In February Magritte was among an audience of about fifteen who attended a lecture on De Stijl given by Van Doesburg at the Centre d'Art.

Magritte painted one of the four portraits of Georges Eekhoud which were presented to him at the Théâtre Lyrique, at Schaerbeek, on March 27 during an evening arranged in his honor by a committee of which Magritte was a member.

Magritte produced cover designs for a monthly review, *Voilà*, which the Bourgeois brothers were hoping to launch in June but which never materialized.

Paul-Gustave van Hecke (1887-1977), the leading artistic impresario of his time in Belgium and Magritte's future dealer, and André de Ridder founded Sélection, under which name they ran a review and, briefly, a gallery. The exhibitions there provided Magritte with opportunities to see the latest avant-garde art from Paris.

In October Magritte attended a congress in Antwerp organized by Jozef Peeters and the architect Huib Hoste for Moderne Kunst, the group Peeters had founded in 1918 with Edmond van Dooren, to provide a link between the avant-garde in Belgium and abroad.

The family moved in November to 16 Avenue du Boulevard, in the Saint-Josse district of Brussels.

Magritte was on active service in the army from December until September 1921. He served in the Tenth Company of the Eighth Regiment. For a while he was stationed in Brussels, during which time he was allowed to continue his studies at the Ecole des Beaux-Arts. After spells in barracks first at Antwerp, then at Leopoldsburg, he was sent to a camp near Aachen in Germany.

Five paintings by Magritte were included in an international exhibition of modern art which opened on December 23 in Geneva.

Poster for Derbaix soup, 1918. Color lithograph, 101 x 36.5 cm. Musées Royaux des Beaux-Arts de Belgique, Brussels

Portrait of Pierre Bourgeois, 1919.
Oil on panel, 40.1 x 34.2 cm.
Communauté française
de Belgique, Bourgeois
Donation

At the Magrittes' home in Brussels, June 1922. First row:
Georgette Magritte, Pierre Broodcorens, Henriette
Flouquet; second row: René Magritte, E. L. T. Mesens,
Victor Servranckx, Pierre-Louis Flouquet, Pierre
Bourgeois

Magritte in his studio, ca. 1920

1921

In November Magritte was given a full-time
job as a designer at Peters-Lacroix, the
wallpaper manufacturer, almost certainly
through Victor Servranckx, the leading
Belgian abstractionist, who had been
employed at the factory since 1918.

1922

In January six paintings by Magritte were
included in the international exhibition that
was part of the second Antwerp Congress
of Modern Art.

Around the beginning of the year Magritte
met Marcel Lecomte (1900–66), one of the
Brussels writers later to become closely
associated with Surrealist activity. He studied
in the Faculty of Letters at the Université Libre
de Bruxelles from 1918 to 1920. His first book,
Démonstrations, was published in Antwerp
by Editions Ça Ira in 1922.

In March Magritte did a final month of
military service, which was spent at Geilen-
kirchen in the German Eifel near Aachen.

Magritte's marriage to Georgette Berger
took place in Brussels on June 28. A nuptial
mass was held at the Eglise de Sainte-Marie,
Schaerbeek, following a civil ceremony at the
Maison Communale of Saint-Josse. In August
they moved into a rented apartment at 7 Rue
Ledeganck, in the Laeken district; Magritte
designed much of the furniture.

The text for a short illustrated book on the
subject of architecture and painting, *L'Art pur:
défense de l'esthétique*, was written by Magritte and
Victor Servranckx towards the end of the year;
though Editions Ça Ira agreed to publish it,
it never appeared. Its content reflects both the
Purist theories of Le Corbusier and Ozenfant
and the late-Cubist theories of Pierre Reverdy.

1923

In January four paintings by Magritte were
included in a young artists' exhibition at the
Galerie Georges Giroux in Brussels. The
exhibitors included Jozef Peeters, Flouquet,
Servranckx, Karel Maes, Marcel Baugniet and
Paul Delvaux.

Magritte showed seven works in an
international exhibition at Antwerp in April
and May organized by the review *Ça Ira*
at the premises of the Cercle Royal Artistique
of Antwerp. The selection was made

by the critic Georges Marlier and included
Baumeister, Feininger, Joostens, Lissitzky,
Moholy-Nagy, Jozef Peeters, Rodchenko
and Servranckx, with those from abroad
represented mainly by graphic work.

At some time in the second half of this year
Magritte was profoundly moved by a
reproduction of De Chirico's *Love Song*, very
probably the one that had appeared in the
Paris review *Les Feuilles libres*, in the issue for
May–June 1923. It was not until the latter part
of 1925 that he started to paint in a way that
reflected this new discovery.

In December Magritte showed four
paintings at the "Salon de la Lanterne
Sourde," two of which were reproduced
in the press. It was the first salon to be
organized by the society La Lanterne Sourde,
which had been founded in 1921 at the
Université Libre de Bruxelles to encourage
cultural exchanges on an international level.

Geert van Bruaene (1891-1964), a former
actor, opened a gallery in Brussels called the
Cabinet Maldoror, where he began a lifelong
practice of dealing in Magritte's work
whenever the occasion arose. By 1926 he had
opened a second gallery in Brussels, La Vierge
Poupine. He was to own many other small
galleries with fanciful names.

It was probably in December that Magritte
met Camille Goemans (1900-60), a civil
servant at the Ministère de l'Industrie et du
Travail and one of the first Brussels writers
to engage in surrealist activity. In July 1924
he published the only book of poems to
appear in his lifetime, *Périples*. In 1926 he went
into partnership with Geert van Bruaene
in the Galerie de la Vierge Poupine and the
following year he started working from Paris
as an independent dealer.

1924

In his search for work as a commercial artist
to replace his job at the wallpaper factory,
which he had left of his own accord, Magritte
tried unsuccessfully in February to find a job
in Paris. He settled for doing freelance
publicity work for clients in Brussels,
in particular for Norine, the leading Brussels
fashion house. It was directed by Honorine
Deschryver (1887-1977), who had founded her
house shortly after the war with her husband
P.-G. van Hecke.

Marcel Mariën, Camille Goemans, Geert van Bruaene, Irène Hamoir, Georgette Magritte,
E. L. T. Mesens, Louis Scutenaire, René Magritte and Paul Colinet in front of Van Bruaene's
bar and gallery La Fleur en Papier Doré. Photograph Albert van Loock, 1953

Portrait of Paul Nougé, 1937. Oil on canvas,
94.3 x 64.5 cm. Musées Royaux des Beaux-
Arts de Belgique, Brussels

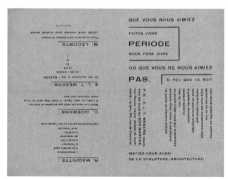

Flyer announcing the Dada review *Période*,
October 1924

Cover for sheet music *Norine Blues*, 1925.
Zincograph, 34.8 x 26.9 cm.
Collection Charly Herscovici, Brussels

The Wreckage of the Dark (*Les Epaves de l'ombre*),
1926. Oil on canvas, 120 x 80 cm.
Musée de Grenoble

In April Magritte received a government grant of 500 Belgian francs, less than the monthly salary he had received at Peters-Lacroix. It was not enough to allow him to devote more time to his painting, of which he did very little in the course of the year.

By the autumn Magritte, largely through Mesens, had become involved in Dada activity and was invited to contribute texts to the final number of Picabia's review *391*. Around the same time, Magritte, Mesens, Lecomte and Goemans issued a prospectus for a Dada review, *Période*. However, only Magritte and Mesens carried on with the project, for the others suddenly deserted them to join Paul Nougé (1895–1967) in producing *Correspondance*, a review in the form of a series of leaflets; twenty-two were published between November 1924 and June 1925. *Correspondance* seized the attention of the Paris Surrealists, and from then on Surrealism was dominated by Nougé, who soon became not only a close friend but a mentor to Magritte. Two thirds of his writings are devoted to Magritte.

1925

In an extensive survey of young Belgian painters in the Brussels monthly review of arts and letters *La Nervie*, for February–March, Magritte was mentioned, along with Victor Servranckx, Pierre Flouquet, Karel Maes and Jozef Peeters, as a "néo-cubiste."

With Magritte and Mesens as co-editors, the Dada review announced the previous October as *Période* appeared in March under the name *Oesophage*. Two further numbers were planned but not published.

Tristan Tzara invited Magritte to send drawings and photographs of paintings for reproduction in the *Little Review* and in an unspecified German magazine. No issue of the *Little Review* contains reproductions of works by Magritte.

"Norine Blues," a song composed by Paul Magritte with lyrics by René and Georgette Magritte (under the pseudonym René Georges), was performed in July at a fashion gala presented by Norine in Ostend. The sheet music was published with a cover design by Magritte.

In October Magritte designed the sets for one-act plays by Herwarth Walden and Max Deauville staged by the Théâtre du Groupe Libre, a recently formed Brussels troupe of young actors committed to modern drama.

In the latter part of this year, following a lull in his painting lasting about two years, Magritte realized his first Surrealist works. The two painters whose influence is most manifest in his new paintings were Max Ernst and Giorgio de Chirico.

In response to Ernst's collages, Magritte also started making papiers collés, and continued to do so until the time of his departure for Paris in September 1927, after which he created very few.

1926

A contract guaranteeing the purchase of Magritte's output was signed in the beginning of the year with P.-G. van Hecke. As of autumn, the Galerie Le Centaure had a half-share in this, and a small part of the production was handled by Camille Goemans. Early in 1929 Van Hecke's share was to be taken over by Le Centaure and that summer the whole contract by Goemans, though only for a matter of months. During his four years under contract Magritte produced about 280 oil paintings, nearly a quarter of his entire production in that medium.

The Magrittes moved in the first weeks of the year to an apartment at 113 Rue Steyls, in the Laeken district of Brussels.

Marie, a new review edited by Mesens, appeared in June and July. Magritte contributed two epigrams to the first issue, a drawing to the second.

Magritte, who was still doing some commercial art, worked throughout the summer on illustrations, incorporating words by Goemans, for the autumn catalogue of S. Samuel et Cie, a Brussels firm of furriers.

When the Galerie Le Centaure moved in October into larger premises on the Avenue Louise, following a merger between Walter Schwarzenberg, its owner, and Blanche Charlet, of the Galerie Charlet, it acquired a half-share in Van Hecke's contract with Magritte and assumed responsibility for exhibiting his work.

In October–November the formation of a Belgian Surrealist group, with Magritte, Mesens, Nougé, Goemans and the composer

André Souris as its nucleus, was heralded by the appearance of three collectively signed texts. The first two, "Quelques turpitudes …" and "Mariés de la Tour Eiffel," were directed against the avant-garde theatre company, the Groupe Libre, for whom Magritte had designed sets the previous year. The third was a catalogue introduction to an exhibition of a naïf painter, Edmond de Crom, at Van Bruaene's gallery, La Vierge Poupine.

1927

In February–March *Adieu à Marie*, edited by Paul Nougé, appeared as a valedictory number of Mesens's review *Marie*. In surrendering editorial control Mesens was acknowledging that Nougé was now in charge of Surrealist activity in Belgium. Magritte's contribution was "Vous," a short text on painting written in the manner of Pascal's *Pensées*.

The March issue of *Sélection* carried the first article published on Magritte, "René Magritte: peintre de la pensée abstraite" by P.-G. van Hecke. It ran to six pages and was accompanied by sixteen full-page illustrations.

Magritte's first one-man show was held at the Galerie Le Centaure, Brussels, from April 23 to May 3. It comprised forty-nine paintings executed since the start of 1926 and twelve papiers collés; the catalogue had prefaces by Nougé and Van Hecke. Press reaction was mainly hostile, notably the long notice in the Constructivist review *7 arts*, by Pierre Flouquet.

Camille Goemans, who had recently gone independent as an art dealer, settled in Paris, probably in April. He lived for a while in Max Ernst's studio in 22 Rue Tourlaque, and eventually found an apartment in the same building, where Joan Miró and Max Morise also had studios. His life in Paris was to be much involved with Magritte's, both as a dealer and as a Surrealist.

In June Magritte met Louis Scutenaire (1905–87), who had recently made himself known to Nougé and Goemans. His first published collection of writings, *Patrimoine ou petite poésie*, appeared in 1927 under the name Jean-Victoire Scutenaire. From the following year he was writing as Jean Scutenaire, after the war as Louis Scutenaire. In 1929 he graduated in law from the Université Libre

in Brussels and was called to the bar in 1930. In February of that year he married the writer and journalist, Irène Hamoir (1906–94), whom he had met in 1928, through Marcel Lecomte.

In the summer Magritte again carried out the illustrations for the annual catalogue of S. Samuel et Cie, furriers. It is a paperback booklet, upright in format, containing sixteen designs, incorporating papier collé. They are reproduced full-page, two of them in color. This time Nougé wrote the words, which consist of short commentaries printed on the pages facing the plates. Both his contribution and Magritte's were anonymous.

Magritte and Nougé also collaborated in the summer on a spoof, *Clarisse Juranville: quelques écrits et quelques dessins*; the purported author had written a standard school manual on the conjugation of verbs.

Around September 10 the Magrittes moved to Paris, renting an apartment on the fifth floor of 101 Avenue de Rosny, Le Perreux-sur-Marne, which lies next to Nogent, to the east of the Château de Vincennes. This remained their address until they returned to Brussels in July 1930. Magritte's youngest brother, Paul, who earned his living mainly by singing at the piano in bars, also moved to Le Perreux, renting a room nearby but spending much of his time at the Avenue de Rosny.

Resuming work around the end of the month, Magritte painted more than thirty canvases by the middle of December. These included his first pictures incorporating words.

An exhibition of contemporary Belgian art at the Musée de Grenoble in September–October included two paintings by Magritte, one of which, *The Wreckage of the Dark (Les Epaves de l'ombre)*, was presented to the museum the following year by the Galerie Le Centaure, thereby becoming his first work to enter a public collection.

In October the Galerie L'Epoque, owned by the Van Heckes, managed by Mesens and specializing in Expressionism and Surrealism, opened on the first floor at 43 Chaussée de Charleroi. It took a more active role than the Galerie Le Centaure in presenting international avant-garde art and here Van Hecke was finally able to market his share of the output of the artists who were under joint contract to him, including Magritte.

Scutenaire and Magritte, ca. 1948–50

Catalogue of Maison Samuel, furriers, 1928. 22 x 15.5 cm. Archives et Musée de la Littérature, Brussels

A one-man show was held at the Galerie L'Epoque, Brussels, from January 7 for about two weeks; it included twenty-three paintings executed in 1927. The brief catalogue preface by Nougé had eight signatories—announcing, in effect, the Brussels Surrealist group.

This was the most fruitful year of Magritte's career. His high rate of production continued and he completed over a hundred paintings, most of which remained unexhibited for several years.

Between February and April three issues appeared of a monthly review, *Distances*, founded by Nougé and Goemans. A fourth issue was planned but a series of misunderstandings and arguments led first to its postponement and then to its demise. Magritte contributed two short texts to the first number, a text and a drawing to the other two.

Throughout most of the year Magritte and Goemans were collaborating intermittently—on a novella, "Les Couleurs de la nuit," which was to occupy them at intervals over the next nine months or more. In 1929 Goemans submitted it to the special Surrealist number of *Variétés* but Breton, one of the guest editors, was unable to accommodate the text, which ran to seven thousand words or more. A shorter, heavily annotated version, discovered among Nougé's papers, was published by Marcel Mariën (Brussels: Les Lèvres Nues, 1978).

Magritte was left out of two major celebrations of Surrealist art in the spring, Breton's book *Le Surréalisme et la peinture* and the "Exposition surréaliste" at the Galerie au Sacre du Printemps, but the acquisition of several of his paintings by Breton later in the year marked his belated acceptance by the Paris Surrealists.

Magritte's father died on August 24 at his home in Brussels. The Magrittes, on hearing that Léopold had suffered a stroke and was gravely ill, had immediately set off for Brussels, but arrived too late.

Towards the end of the year Magritte's painting began to attempt a crisper illusion of reality, involving an increasingly polished realization; this was accompanied by a marked decrease in the rate of his output.

Paul Magritte posing between three paintings and a drawing by his brother René, Le Perreux-sur-Marne, 1928. From top to bottom: Sketch for *Figure Brooding on Madness* (*Personnage méditant sur la folie*), *Reclining Nude* (*Le Nu couché*), *The Use of Speech* (*L'Usage de la parole*) and *The Disguised Symbol* (*Le Symbole dissimulé*)

Drawing by Magritte in *Distances*, 1928

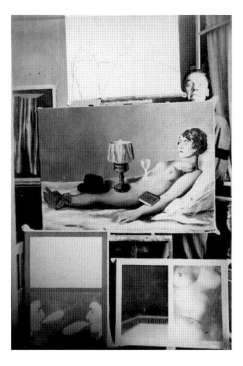

Magritte with *The Empty Mask* (*Le Masque vide*), Le Perreux-sur-Marne, 1928

1929

The January 15 issue of *Variétés* reproduced several works by Magritte, one of them on the cover. Its editor was P.-G. van Hecke, Magritte's dealer.

On January 20 a one-day, one-man show of eighteen paintings from 1926–8 was hung at the Salle de la Bourse, Charleroi, in conjunction with a recital of modern music conducted by André Souris. It was introduced by Nougé, who expressly defended music against detractors such as De Chirico and the Paris Surrealists.

The Galerie L'Epoque and its share of Magritte's contract were taken over in late January by the Galerie Le Centaure, a deal which had vital consequences for Magritte as well as for Van Hecke and Mesens. In the mounting general financial crisis L'Epoque was to survive for only three more months.

In February–March Magritte and Goemans brought out a series of leaflets, *Le Sens propre*, each reproducing a painting above a poem written to go with it; five were published, dated at weekly intervals from February 16 to March 16. The leaflet form was an economical alternative to the original intention which had been to publish the work as a book.

Magritte was among the artists and intellectuals who accepted the invitation issued by Breton and Aragon to respond to the questionnaire which they circulated in February concerning the critical and divisive problem of collective political action and the further invitation to attend a meeting on March 11 at the Bar du Château. Magritte's reply established him as a partisan of collective action.

In the spring Magritte met Salvador Dalí, who was in Paris for the making of *Un Chien andalou*. The meeting took place at Goemans's apartment. A series of reports which Dalí wrote about the Paris art world for a Catalan-language newspaper, *La Publicitat* (Barcelona), before returning to Spain at the end of May or beginning of June included several references to Magritte.

A special number of *Variétés*, "Le Surréalisme en 1929," which was edited by Breton and Aragon, appeared on June 1. It included the momentous "A suivre," the report which Breton and Aragon had prepared on the subject of their questionnaire of February 12, 1929, and the subsequent meeting at the Bar du Château. Two reproductions of works by Magritte were included in addition to a drawing.

In July Magritte's contract with Le Centaure suddenly terminated while sales of his work by Goemans suddenly increased. The stock of Magrittes which had accumulated at Le Centaure was to stay intact until the gallery's liquidation in 1932.

The Magrittes spent August in Cadaqués, on the Catalonian coast, at the suggestion of Dalí, who was staying there at his family's summer house; others there at his suggestion were Goemans and Yvonne Bernard, who shared a rented house with the Magrittes, and Paul and Gala Eluard. It was during this holiday that Gala Eluard left her husband for Dalí and Magritte's lifelong friendship with Eluard started to flourish.

The Galerie Goemans opened at 49 Rue de Seine, Paris, in October with an inaugural exhibition of works by the artists under contract: Arp, Dalí, Tanguy and Magritte. The month the gallery opened was the month of the Wall Street Crash. Its short life encompassed only three further formal exhibitions—a one-man Arp show in November, a highly successful Dalí show and the famous anthology of collages organized the following year in collaboration with Louis Aragon.

La Révolution surréaliste, no. 12, dated December 15, 1929, included four contributions from Magritte: the most famous of his writings, the illustrated set of propositions, "Les Mots et les images"; a small collage; his reply to the survey on love; and a full-page montage presenting one of his paintings *The Hidden Woman* (*La Femme cachée*; private collection) framed by photographs of Surrealist artists and writers.

At a gathering in his apartment on December 14 there was a clash between the Magrittes and Breton. Breton had noticed that Georgette was wearing a cross on a chain and demanded its removal. Georgette preferred to leave and Magritte went with her. This brought about an estrangement from the Paris Surrealists which lasted for more than two years.

Le Sens propre, February–March 1929

Special number of *Variétés*, "Le Surréalisme en 1929," June 1929. Koninklijk Museum voor Schone Kunsten, Antwerp

The Seers (*Les Voyantes*). Photograph, 1930. Marthe Nougé and Georgette Magritte

135 Rue Esseghem, Brussels

1930

Magritte painted several major works for a one-man exhibition at the Galerie Goemans scheduled for early March; the exhibition never opened and the paintings remained with Magritte until he sold them to Mesens in the summer.

Magritte was represented in a major exhibition of collages at the Galerie Goemans from March 28 to April 12. It was organized by Goemans and Aragon, whose classic text, "La Peinture au défi," was written as the preface to the catalogue.

Magritte was left without a dealer when the Galerie Goemans closed down in the latter part of April. The closure was the culmination of a crisis precipitated by Goemans's loss of his mistress, Yvonne Bernard, to his Dutch backer, Rott. In May Goemans moved back to Brussels. Magritte stopped painting and started looking for work as a commercial artist.

In June Magritte negotiated the sale to Mesens of the eleven paintings left on his hands.

Early in July the Magrittes moved back to Brussels. They rented an apartment in the Jette district, at 135 Rue Esseghem, where they were to live until 1954.

Financially dependent again on commercial art, Magritte set up a business in a shed-like studio in the garden at 135 Rue Esseghem doing publicity and display work under the name Studio Dongo. His brother Paul ran the business side, his other brother, Raymond, used his business contacts to get commissions and other members of the family helped out. Magritte's comparatively small output of fine art between the middle of 1930 and the end of 1934—less than fifty oils and less than a dozen gouaches—reflected the heavy demands the commercial work made on his time.

1931

Magritte was represented in "L'Art vivant en Belgique 1910-1930" at the Galerie Georges Giroux, Brussels, which ran from January 17-28. This was the first exhibition to be organized by L'Art Vivant, a society newly formed to champion contemporary art.

A one-man exhibition of sixteen paintings from 1927-30 opened at the Salle Giso, the premises of a firm of Brussels interior decorators, on February 9. It was organized by Mesens and the owner of the firm, Ewold van Tonderen, as a salute to Magritte to mark his return to Brussels. The catalogue was by Nougé. There was a spectacular all-night preview.

Magritte exhibited for the first of many times at the Palais des Beaux-Arts, Brussels, when he was represented in April–May in a major international exhibition, "L'Art vivant en Europe." This was organized by L'Art Vivant together with La Société Auxiliaire des Expositions du Palais des Beaux-Arts, which was run by Claude Spaak, the novelist and playwright, who in the course of the 1930s was to become the main private collector of both Magritte and Paul Delvaux. He was assisted at the Palais des Beaux-Arts by several other supporters of Magritte including Robert Giron and E. L. T. Mesens.

Twenty-seven paintings and three gouaches executed between 1926 and 1931 were shown at the Palais des Beaux-Arts, Brussels, from December 19 to January 6 in a three-man exhibition with René Guiette and David-Olivier Picard organized by L'Art Vivant.

1932

Magritte was among the signatories to *La Poésie transfigurée*, a tract written by Nougé and published in January, which set out the position of the Belgian Surrealists on the urgent issue raised by the Paris group in *L'Affaire Aragon*, the tract issued by them in protest against the indictment of Aragon on January 16 over the publication of his poem "Front rouge."

In the spring Magritte collaborated with Nougé on two short films, the earliest of many home movies Magritte was to be involved in making.

Nearly two hundred works by Magritte from the years 1926-9 were included in the liquidation of the Galerie Le Centaure's stock in the autumn of 1932 and of P.-G. van Hecke's collection in 1932-3. The vast majority were acquired by Mesens and Spaak. These liquidations greatly affected the accessibility to the public of the work from Magritte's Paris period, most of which had not been exhibited.

The Shadow and Its Shadow (*L'Ombre et son ombre*). Photograph, 1932. René and Georgette Magritte, Rue Esseghem, Brussels

Advertisement for *Persan Bitter de marque*, 1932. Color lithograph, 30 x 40 cm

Violette Nozières, Brussels: Editions Nicolas Flamel, 1933. Private collection

Cover for sheet music *Marie Trombone Chapeau Buse* (1936). Zincograph, 35.1 x 27.2 cm. Archives de l'Art contemporain en Belgique, Brussels

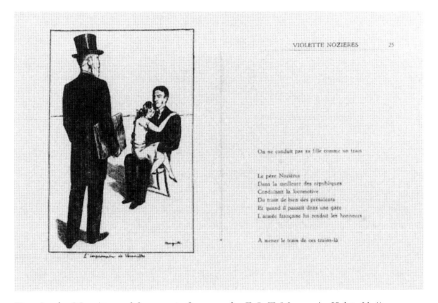

Drawing by Magritte and fragment of a poem by E. L. T. Mesens in *Violette Nozières*, Brussels: Editions Nicolas Flamel, 1933

Early in the year Magritte began devising images in a way he considered to be a radical innovation: the method was to search out the "solution" to the "problem" posed by a given type of object. The point of departure was *Elective Affinities* (*Les Affinités électives*; Collection E. Perier, Paris), while the first works in which the method was deliberately used were *The Unexpected Answer* (*La Réponse imprévue*; Musées Royaux des Beaux-Arts de Belgique, Brussels) and *The Human Condition* (*La Condition humaine*; National Gallery of Art, Washington, DC).

In April Magritte was invited by Breton to contribute to *Le Surréalisme au service de la révolution*, a gesture that signaled an end to the estrangement that had existed between them since December 1929. Nos. 5 and 6, the two final issues of the review published simultaneously in Paris on May 15, carried reproductions of his work and a text on him by Nougé. His reconciliation with the Paris Surrealists was also marked by his inclusion in their major group exhibition at the Galerie Pierre Colle and in their showing as a group within the Salon des Surindépendants.

A one-man show was held at the Palais des Beaux-Arts, Brussels, from May 27 to June 7. Of the fifty-seven paintings, only eight had been executed since 1930; the others dated from 1926–9 but had never been exhibited. The inclusion of two painted ready-made plaster casts constituted the first showing, accompanied in Nougé's preface by the first published discussion, of a kind of object which Magritte had been realizing for some time.

Magritte contributed one of the drawings in the booklet *Violette Nozières*, assembled by the Paris Surrealists and published in Brussels on December 1. Violette Nozière was a schoolgirl who had been arrested in a Paris café on August 28 for the murder of her father, Baptiste, and the attempted murder of her mother, Germaine.

In the course of 1933 Magritte got to know the writer and poet Paul Colinet (1898–1957), who became closely involved with the Brussels Surrealists' activities. His first publication was the setting of his poem "Marie trombone chapeau buse" to music by Paul Magritte, which appeared with a cover drawing by Magritte in 1936.

1934

In February–March Magritte was represented in a major international exhibition at the Palais des Beaux-Arts, Brussels, "Le Nu dans l'art vivant," organized jointly by L'Art Vivant and the Société Auxiliaire des Expositions du Palais des Beaux-Arts. It had a hundred paintings and sculptures by nineteenth- and twentieth-century artists.

Magritte was represented in an exhibition celebrating the first anniversary of the review *Minotaure*, organized by its publishers, Editions Albert Skira, Paris, and shown at the Palais des Beaux-Arts, Brussels, from May 12 to June 3. The idea of putting it on in Brussels seems to have originated with Eluard.

Magritte was among the key contributors to "Intervention surréaliste," a special number of the Brussels quarterly *Documents 34*, published in June. Mesens was the editor of this issue and of the next, which was likewise dominated by the Surrealists. Eluard played a very active role in putting together the special number, the contributors to which included Breton, Péret, Dalí, Crevel and Tzara, as well as himself. The Brussels and Paris Surrealists had not collaborated so closely since the special Surrealist issue of *Variétés* in June 1929.

Breton's lecture on Surrealism, given to mark the special Surrealist issue of *Documents 34*, was delivered in Brussels on June 1, 1934, and published there on July 15 as *Qu'est-ce que le Surréalisme?* with a cover designed by Magritte. At the same time Breton told Magritte that he was planning to write about him. Although Magritte sent him photographs with a cover letter which contained important remarks about several recent works, nothing resulted.

1935

There was a sharp increase this year in Magritte's output, partly owing to the patronage of Claude Spaak. It was also stimulated by the prospect of a one-man show in New York for which Magritte produced, for the first time, a quantity of replicas and variants of existing images, mainly on a small scale. Meanwhile, exhibiting in Belgium was confined to mixed shows.

Magritte was one of the twenty-six signatories to *Du temps que les Surréalistes avaient*

raison, the tract published in Paris in August which marked the Surrealists' break with the Communist Party. Magritte's personal position regarding the Party had been that of a fellow-traveler, although his commitment to Communist principles had been avowed unambiguously in May of this year in the course of a reply to a questionnaire organized by Paul Fierens on the current crisis in painting. He does not seem to have become a member of the Party until 1945.

The *Bulletin international du Surréalisme*, no. 3, was published in Brussels on August 20 with a gouache by Magritte on the cover. It included the tract *Le Couteau dans la plaie* —an attack on the nationalism manifest in the recent Franco-Soviet pact—to which Magritte was one of the signatories.

A poem by Paul Eluard, "René Magritte," was published in *Cahiers d'art* (Paris), nos. 5–6, in the autumn together with a text and two paintings by Magritte. The poem was reprinted the following year in Eluard's volume, *Les Yeux fertiles*, and an English translation by Man Ray was published in the catalogue of Magritte's one-man show at the Julien Levy Gallery, New York, in 1936.

Magritte was included in the Surrealist exhibition organized by Mesens at La Louvière from October 13 to 27 to mark the formation of a Surrealist group in Hainaut (the province south of Brussels where Magritte grew up). On the day of the opening there was a "Manifestation surréaliste" consisting of a lecture by Mesens on Surrealism, readings by Irène Hamoir and Mesens and texts set to music by Souris.

Around the turn of the year Mesens began to act on Magritte's behalf in the marketing of his work abroad.

1936

Magritte had his first one-man show in America at the Julien Levy Gallery, New York, from January 3 to 20. It consisted of twenty-two paintings, two dating from the late 1920s, the remainder new works of which fifteen were small replicas or variants on earlier images. Nothing was sold from the exhibition apart from five works bought by Levy himself.

Magritte was one of seventeen signatories to a tract dated January 21, *Le Domestique zélé*, announcing the expulsion of André Souris

André Breton, *Qu'est-ce que le Surréalisme?*, Brussels: René Henriquez, 1934

Deep Waters (*Les Eaux profondes*), 1934. Photograph. Georgette Magritte, Rue Esseghem, Brussels

from the Belgian Surrealist group. He had offended the Surrealists' anticlerical principles by agreeing to conduct an orchestra at a Mass. In marked contrast with the ways of the Paris Surrealists, the expulsions of Marcel Lecomte (in 1926) and Souris were the only ones imposed throughout the history of Surrealism in Belgium.

A one-man show was held at the Palais des Beaux-Arts, Brussels, from April 25 to May 6. The works are listed in the catalogue in three groups: thirty paintings, two "tableaux-objets" and three "objets." The exhibition occasioned the publication of "René Magritte ou La révélation objective" in *Les Beaux-Arts* (Brussels), May 1, an anonymous set of poetic commentaries on seven paintings ascribed there to Magritte's friends but largely written by Nougé who absorbed ideas from several contributors and used many of his own.

Magritte was represented by three works in the "Exposition surréaliste d'objets," the historic exhibition organized by Breton and other leading Paris Surrealists which took place at Charles Ratton's gallery in Paris from May 22 to 29.

Magritte was represented by eight oils and six works on paper in the first major international Surrealist exhibition, held in London at the New Burlington Galleries from June 11 to July 4. Mesens played a crucial role in the installation of the show.

A one-man show was held at a small commercial gallery in The Hague, the Huize Esher Surrey, from November 14 to December 5. It presented a retrospective selection of twenty paintings and six gouaches.

Magritte was represented by ten works in the major international show organized by Alfred Barr, "Fantastic art, Dada, Surrealism," which opened on December 8 at the Museum of Modern Art, New York.

There was a sudden increase in Magritte's output of gouaches this year which never subsequently slackened. Generally the gouaches were of images also realized as paintings, usually with the painting but sometimes the gouache coming first. This was due to his exploitation of successful images by repeating them on a smaller scale as opportunities for exhibiting his work increased.

Marcel Mariën, Magritte, Louis Scutenaire, Paul Nougé and Noël Arnaud, November 1947

1937

In February–March Magritte stayed with Edward James at his London house for four or five weeks in order to carry out a commission from him for three large paintings. During his stay he gave a lecture at the London Gallery.

In July Magritte met Marcel Mariën (b. 1920), a young writer from Antwerp. Their friendship, which is documented in a series of 278 letters from Magritte published by Mariën in 1977, lasted until 1954.

In an exhibition of "Trois peintres surréalistes: René Magritte, Man Ray, Yves Tanguy" at the Palais des Beaux-Arts, Brussels, from December 11 to 22, Magritte showed a selection of twenty paintings and four works on paper. The catalogue text consists of a general introduction by Scutenaire entitled "Trois fenêtres," reprints of a poem by Eluard and an epigram by Breton on each artist.

1938

Magritte had his second one-man show at the Julien Levy Gallery, New York, from January 4 to 18. It presented a retrospective selection of sixteen paintings.

Magritte was one of the half-dozen painters most amply represented in the "Exposition internationale du Surréalisme" at the Galerie Beaux-Arts, Paris, in January–February 1938. This was the greatest of the Surrealist exhibitions, organized by Breton and Eluard in consultation with Duchamp. Magritte went to Paris for the opening on January 17.

The London Gallery, having been taken over by Mesens and Roland Penrose, reopened on the eve of April 1 with a one-man show of Magritte, a retrospective selection of thirty-three paintings, four objects and nine works on paper. The catalogue was subsumed into the inaugural issue of the *London Bulletin*, which was mainly devoted to Magritte.

Having failed to persuade Edward James to provide him with a small regular income, Magritte turned to Mesens and over the next six months was involved in an acrimonious contract negotiation with him.

Magritte delivered a lecture, "La Ligne de vie," at the Koninklijk Museum voor Schone Kunsten in Antwerp on the morning of Sunday, November 20, to an audience of around five hundred. It was the most revealing account he was ever to set down of his experience as an artist.

1939

A one-man show of recent work at the Palais des Beaux-Arts, Brussels, from May 13 to 24, consisted of ten paintings and twenty-four gouaches, reflecting an upsurge in Magritte's use of gouache, especially to realize images never executed in oil. The catalogue had a preface by Nougé.

In the course of the year, Magritte's sister-in-law, Léontine Berger-Hoyez, opened La Maison Berger, a shop specializing in artists' materials, which henceforth supplied Magritte with all his canvases and paints. Georgette Magritte worked there part-time until the mid-1950s.

1940

A new Surrealist review in which Magritte played a central part, *L'Invention collective*, appeared in February and in April. The absence of any editorial credit reflects the collective spirit expressed in the title. Magritte shared the administrative burden with Raoul Ubac, the painter and photographer, who had returned to Belgium from Paris in the autumn of 1939.

Five days after the Germans invaded Belgium and Holland on May 10, Magritte left for France leaving Georgette behind. He traveled as far as Paris in the company of the Scutenaires and the Ubacs. By May 23 he was in Carcassonne where he was joined by the Scutenaires in the second half of June. He returned to Brussels around August 10.

Nineteen works by Magritte stored in a London depository by the directors of the London Gallery, E. L. T. Mesens and Roland Penrose, were destroyed in the autumn by bombing.

1941

A one-man show of fifteen recent paintings and five drawings was held at Walter Schwarzenberg's new gallery, the Galerie Dietrich, Brussels, from January 4 to 22.

1942

Lou Cosyn, who had lately opened a gallery in Brussels, the running of which was helped

Page from the manuscript of "La Ligne de vie," 1938. Private collection

Cover design for the review *L'Invention collective*, April 1940. China ink on paper, 16.5 x 11.8 cm. Musées Royaux des Beaux-Arts de Belgique, Brussels

Drawing for Paul Eluard's poem *Moralité du sommeil*, 1941. China ink on paper, 17.8 x 12.9 cm. Musées Royaux des Beaux-Arts de Belgique, Brussels

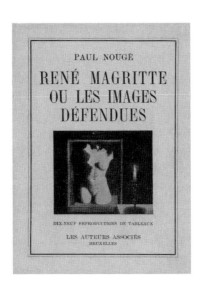

Paul Nougé, *René Magritte ou Les Images défendues*. Brussels: Les Auteurs associés, 1943

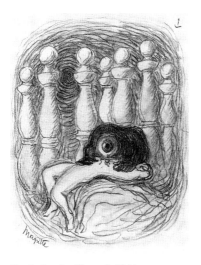

Study for *Les Chants de Maldoror*, 1945. Crayon on paper, 25 x 18 cm. The Menil Collection, Houston

by her lover, later her husband, Camille Goemans, started to purchase works from Magritte, whose principal dealer she was to be over the next five years.

Magritte compiled the documentation for a monograph on him by Louis Scutenaire, including a sketchy year-by-year list of the titles of his works. The book was published in 1947 by the Librairie Sélection, Brussels, with the title *René Magritte*.

The first film about Magritte, based on a scenario by Nougé and directed by Robert Cocriamont, was probably made in August. Entitled *Rencontre de René Magritte*, it is part of *Images de Flandres*, a black-and-white silent picture on 16 mm lasting 20 minutes and featuring four Belgian painters (the others are Gustave de Smet, Edgard Tytgat and Paul Delvaux).

1943

In April, prompted by a concern he had been feeling under the Occupation to make pictures that would radiate a sense of pleasure, Magritte began adopting the palette and handling of the Impressionists, especially Renoir. Over the next four years he was to produce seventy-odd oils and nearly fifty gouaches in this style, while sometimes, especially in 1945, reverting to his usual manner.

A private showing of recent paintings was held on July 10, 11 and 17 at Lou Cosyn's gallery in Brussels. Like other events organized by Lou Cosyn and Camille Goemans under the Occupation, it was a semi-clandestine affair in order to avoid the vigilance of German censorship.

The first monograph on Magritte was published in Brussels in August, with an introductory essay by Marcel Mariën. Eight examples of his new manner were included in Magritte's choice of the twenty paintings reproduced. All the plates were in color and it has been alleged by Mariën that they were paid for by Magritte's making and selling of forgeries.

René Magritte ou les Images défendues by Paul Nougé, a book which had been largely composed by 1933, appeared in October in Brussels with nineteen black-and-white plates. Several sections had been included in *Le Surréalisme au service de la révolution*, no. 5,

in May 1933. Magritte's alteration of the original title, *Les Images défendues*, was never forgiven by Nougé.

1944

A one-man show of about twenty recent paintings was held at the Galerie Dietrich, Brussels, from January 8 to 22. It constituted the first public showing of Magritte's "Impressionist" work—versus the private exhibition of it at Lou Cosyn's the summer before. The exhibition and the catalogue preface by Nougé were attacked in the press by a former ally, Marc Eemans, who had become a supporter of the Nazis' war on "degenerate art."

Magritte was commissioned for the first time to produce a set of book illustrations, twelve drawings for William Beckford's *Vathek*: the edition was never published.

Magritte was visited towards the end of the year by Jacques Wergifosse (b. 1928), a sixteen-year-old poet from Liège who became his friend and disciple.

1945

In the course of the first half of the year, Magritte produced a set of pen-and-ink drawings to illustrate Lautréamont's *Les Chants de Maldoror*, using a style adapted from his "Impressionist" style of painting. Around the turn of the year he made similar drawings for a volume of Eluard poems, *Les Nécessités de la vie et les conséquences des rêves précédé d'Exemples*, first published in 1921 in Paris by Au Sans Pareil. Shortly afterwards he made a set of drawings for an edition of Bataille's recent novel, *Madame Edwarda*, which never appeared, and another set, published posthumously, for a book on the Marquis de Sade by Gaston Puel.

The issue dated September 8–9 of the Brussels Communist daily *Le Drapeau rouge* announced that Magritte had joined the Belgian Communist Party. After about eighteen months his enthusiasm for the Party waned, though his faith in Communism did not.

A large, mainly Belgian, Surrealist exhibition, principally organized by Magritte, was held at the Galerie des Editions de la Boétie, Brussels, from December 15 to January 15, 1946. The role played by Magritte in its realization reflected the position he had come to have as the leader of the Surrealist movement in Belgium.

1946

In February Magritte was approached with a view to an exhibition at the Hugo Gallery, 26 East 55th Street, New York, whose director, Alexander Iolas, was soon to become his lifelong agent.

In the spring and summer Magritte was heavily engaged, together with Nougé and especially Mariën, in producing and distributing a number of publications: three anonymous tracts, *L'Imbécile*, *L'Emmerdeur* and *L'Enculeur*, most of the copies of which were seized by the postal authorities; a hoax prospectus for a lecture series by a Bulgarian sexologist with live demonstrations which provoked a frantic demand for tickets; and then five small books—a volume of poems by Jacques Wergifosse, polemical texts by Nougé and Mariën, the anonymous *Dix tableaux de Magritte précédés de descriptions*, and an enquiry into personal likes and dislikes, *Le Savoir Vivre*, which involved Magritte in some exacting editorial work.

In June Magritte made his first trip to Paris since the war. He was accompanied by Mariën and stayed for a week, renewing contact with old friends such as Breton and Picabia and trying to set up an exhibition.

In the latter half of the year Magritte was heavily engaged, through correspondence with Breton and the composition of a tract, in trying to muster support for his personal concept of the future of Surrealism, *Le Surréalisme en plein soleil*.

A one-man show of twenty-three recent works comprising eight paintings, thirteen gouaches and two drawings was held at the Galerie Dietrich, Brussels, from November 30 to December 11. Magritte conceived of it as a demonstration on behalf of "Sunlit Surrealism" and Nougé's polemical catalogue preface was written to serve that purpose. Magritte subsequently wrote a set of brief commentaries on the titles of the works.

1947

A one-man show in Verviers, at the Société Royale des Beaux-Arts, from January 19 to February 2, comprised thirty-one or more

 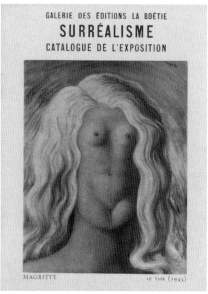

Poster for the exhibition "Surréalisme," Galerie des Editions de la Boétie, Brussels, December 15, 1945–January 15, 1946

Catalogue of the exhibition "Surréalisme," Galerie des Editions de la Boétie, Brussels, December 15, 1945–January 15, 1946

Four drawings for Gaston Puel's book, *Le Marquis de Sade*, and a letter to Puel, dated July 13, 1946. Private collection, Antwerp

The Depths of Pleasure (*Les Profondeurs du plaisir*), 1948. Gouache on paper, 46 x 32.8 cm. Musées Royaux des Beaux-Arts de Belgique, Brussels

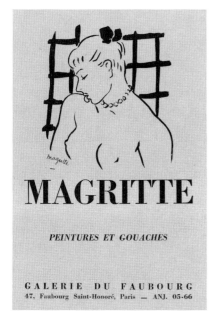

Poster for the exhibition "Magritte. Peintures et gouaches," Galerie du Faubourg, Paris, May 11–June 5, 1948

canvases of the "Impressionist" period and five earlier paintings. The catalogue introduction was by Jacques Wergifosse.

The first of the one-man shows to be staged by Alexander Iolas took place at his gallery in New York, the Hugo Gallery, from April 7 to 30. Eighteen paintings dating from 1926 onwards, twenty-one recent gouaches and six drawings are listed in the catalogue; but, as a result of Magritte's ignorance of US Customs regulations, ten of the gouaches and the six drawings were missing from the exhibition.

A one-man show of new work at the Galerie Lou Cosyn, Brussels, from May 31 to June 21, consisted of thirty very small gouaches, half of them variations on a single theme, *Shéhérazade*, and a few paintings. These works included the final products of Magritte's "Impressionist" style.

The international exhibition of Surrealism at the Galerie Maeght in Paris, which opened on July 7, gave Breton the opportunity publicly to condemn Magritte's concept of "le Surréalisme en plein soleil" and thus to signal his excommunication.

The monograph by Louis Scutenaire, largely composed five years before, was published in Brussels in August.

Magritte contributed two paintings to a large international exhibition organized by L'Amicale des Artistes Communistes de Belgique, which took place from October 11 to 25 at the Maison de la Presse Communiste, 33 Rue de la Caserne, the premises of the daily newspaper, *Le Drapeau rouge*. He subsequently issued a strong protest against the Party newspaper's deferential report of a royal visit to the show.

1948

A one-man show of about fifteen recent paintings at the Galerie Dietrich, Brussels, from January 24 to February 4, reflected Magritte's abandonment of his "Impressionist" style. Nougé's preface, which was a continuation of the battle with Breton, was to be his final text on Magritte.

In the course of the year a basis was established for Iolas's dealings with Magritte. A one-man show of recent work, comprising seventeen oils and about fifteen gouaches, opened at Iolas's Hugo Gallery, New York,

on May 4. In September a one-man show staged as the inaugural exhibition of the Copley Galleries in Beverly Hills, California, consisted of eleven of those paintings and six earlier ones with a selection of twelve gouaches.

Magritte's first one-man exhibition in Paris was held from May 11 to June 5 at a minor dealer's gallery, the Galerie du Faubourg. The works, done for the occasion in about five weeks, were in a flamboyant, vivid, caricatural style dubbed "vache": the catalogue lists fifteen of the seventeen such oils that were executed and ten of the twenty-two or more gouaches. Magritte's adoption of this style, which pushed his cult of pleasure to a violent extreme, was a provocation, and Scutenaire's catalogue preface, "Les Pieds dans le plat," was correspondingly slangy and aggressive. The exhibition was coolly received, nothing was sold, and Magritte resigned himself to a future of exhibiting work in his usual style.

1949

An exhibition of recent work at the Galerie Lou Cosyn, Brussels, was held from February 12 to March 2.

In mid-February Iolas visited Magritte to discuss future plans, and during a further visit in August an agreement was reached on a list of new works for the Hugo Gallery, and these were despatched the following month.

1950

Following some quarrelsome correspondence between Magritte and Iolas and the postponement of an exhibition planned for April, a visit from Iolas at the end of May resolved their disagreements. The exhibition was rescheduled for September and a selection made of new works, which were despatched to New York in mid-August.

A proposal Magritte put forward in June, by which the Hugo Gallery was to have sole rights to his production in return for a yearly salary, was not taken up.

In December, despite the postponement yet again of his exhibition, Magritte arranged for a further consignment of paintings to be delivered to the Hugo Gallery at the very end of the year.

1951

An exhibition of about forty works opened at Iolas's gallery in New York on March 21.

An exhibition of twenty-seven recent works was held at the Galeries Dietrich et Lou Cosyn, Brussels, from April 7 to 18.

1952

Magritte's first retrospective since the war was held at the Casino Communal at Knokke-le-Zoute, from August 2 to 22: it was apparently organized by Mesens, who had recently re-established business activities in Brussels following the closure of the London Gallery in July 1950.

In September Magritte broke off his friendship with Paul Nougé.

In October Magritte founded *La Carte d'après nature*, a review which was to appear at irregular intervals until April 1956, generally in the form of a postcard.

1953

Magritte's first exhibition in Italy, consisting of twelve oils and sixteen gouaches, was held at a small gallery in Rome, the Galleria dell'Obelisco, from January 19 to February 2. He was also attempting at this time to find other outlets for the sale of his work in Europe, including L'Etoile Scellée, André Breton's new gallery in Paris. He offered work for sale in no less than twelve exhibitions, half of them one-man shows, in Belgium and elsewhere between autumn 1952 and spring 1954.

In March an exhibition of Magritte's work opened at the Iolas Gallery, New York.

In April, having submitted sketches executed in gouache, Magritte was commissioned by Gustave Nellens, proprietor of the Casino at Knokke-le-Zoute, to decorate its Salle du Lustre with a panoramic mural. In May he produced eight oil paintings as models, and in June these designs were realized on the wall by a team of painters working under his supervision.

In November Magritte met George Balanchine at Iolas's instigation to discuss the possibility of collaboration on a ballet. As it turned out Balanchine did not show much enthusiasm for the collaboration and the idea was quietly dropped.

Magritte supervising work on *The Enchanted Domain* (*Le Domaine enchanté*), Casino Communal, Knokke-le-Zoute, 1953

A collaborator working on one of the sections of *The Enchanted Domain* (*Le Domaine enchanté*), 1953

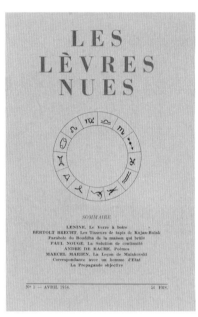

Les Lèvres nues, no. 1, April 1954

Still from the short film *The West-Indian Dessert* (*Le Dessert des Antilles*), 1957

Still from the short film *The Red Wolf* (*Le Loup rouge*), 1960

1954

"Word vs. image," an exhibition of twenty-one word-pictures executed by Magritte between 1927 and 1930, was held at the Sidney Janis Gallery, New York, from March 1 to 20. Although the show had no commercial success, it helped to focus American critical attention on what later proved to be one of the most influential aspects of Magritte's art.

In April Marcel Mariën founded a review, *Les Lèvres Nues*, which hastened the end of his friendship with Magritte.

The first major retrospective of Magritte's work, consisting of nearly a hundred paintings, was held at the Palais des Beaux-Arts, Brussels, from May 7 to June 1. The catalogue, edited by Mesens, contained two important texts written for the occasion by Magritte.

In May the Magrittes moved to an apartment on the ground floor of 207 Boulevard de Lambermont in the Schaerbeek district of Brussels.

A retrospective selection of twenty-four works by Magritte was included in the Belgian pavilion of the Venice Biennale, which ran from June 19 to October 17 and took Surrealism as a main theme.

1955

In the course of trying to find a gallery to give him a one-man show in Paris, Magritte unwittingly became the focus of a dispute among young followers of Breton. A show was eventually arranged at Zervos's Galerie "Cahiers d'Art," opening on December 21. It contained ten paintings and ten gouaches and was quite well received by the critics, although no works were sold.

In December, following the death of their dog, the Magrittes moved up the street to a ground-floor apartment at 404 Boulevard de Lambermont.

1956

In March the Cercle Royal Artistique et Littéraire de Charleroi marked the occasion of their thirtieth Salon with a Magritte retrospective including more than a hundred works, all from Belgian collections.

On March 28 Magritte was commissioned to produce a mural for the Salle des Congrès in the new Palais des Beaux-Arts in Charleroi.

He submitted his plan for the mural in June, and it was approved by the council, but not unanimously (one member resigned in protest), and the mural was executed in March–April 1957.

In the spring Magritte met Barnet Hodes, a successful Chicago lawyer with a keen interest in Surrealism and in collecting, who over the next ten years commissioned more than fifty gouaches and papiers collés, mostly replicas and variations of existing images.

In October Magritte bought a ciné camera and began to make short films—Surrealist home movies—featuring himself, Georgette, Louis Scutenaire, Irène Hamoir, Paul Colinet and other friends. Most were shot in black-and-white but at least two were shot in color; some were destroyed by Magritte himself, a few appear to have been severely cut by others, probably in the course of editing them for commercial purposes.

On December 24, in the course of one of Iolas's periodic visits to Magritte, they agreed to the terms of a contract which gave Iolas exclusive rights to virtually all Magritte's work for the following year, with a provision for indefinite renewal.

1957

Magritte's first one-man show in four years at the Iolas Gallery, New York, opened on March 25. In this first year of their contract Iolas was much more forceful in his suggestions of the work Magritte should be doing, and three of the ten oils sent off in December for an exhibition at the Galerie "Cahiers d'Art" in January were in a large format that Iolas had requested.

On March 8 Magritte was elected to the Libre Académie de Belgique in place of Pierre Bourgeois who had recently retired.

In October Magritte met Harry Torczyner, a leading New York lawyer born and educated in Antwerp, who was to become a legal adviser, a major collector of his work, a close friend and the author of a monograph on him.

In November Maurice Rapin and Mirabelle Dors, two French disciples of Magritte, published, under the imprint "La Tendance Populaire Surréaliste," the first of a number of tracts on the painter largely based upon extracts from his letters to them and each illustrated with one of his works.

Magritte filming, 1959

The Magrittes' last residence, 97 Rue des Mimosas, Schaerbeek (Brussels)

Magritte during the shooting of Luc de Heusch's film
Magritte ou la leçon des choses, 1959

Harry Torczyner and Suzi Gablik, 1960

Suzi Gablik Reading, 1960–61.
Drawing. Whereabouts
unknown

Magritte's close friend, Paul Colinet, died
of cancer on December 23.

The Magrittes changed addresses for the
last time on December 24 when they moved
into a detached house with a garden, which
they began by renting but were later to
purchase, at 97 Rue des Mimosas in the
Schaerbeek district of Brussels.

1958.

During one of his most prolific years,
Magritte not only produced a full set of work
for Iolas but also executed a number of works
for other clients, only some of which Iolas
knew about.

In July Magritte began corresponding
with a young poet in Liège, André Bosmans
(b. 1938), with whom he remained friendly for
the rest of his life.

1959

In March Iolas arranged two simultaneous
exhibitions in New York of Magritte's latest
work, with paintings at his own gallery and
drawings at the Bodley Gallery. He also
encouraged him to do more large variants
of old paintings, but Magritte resisted this
pressure, and his output during the year
of both variants and new works was
significantly reduced.

A retrospective, mainly consisting of works
in Belgian collections, was held at the Musée
d'Ixelles, Brussels, from April 19 to May 16.

For several weeks in July and August
Magritte was involved in the making of a
fifteen-minute 35 mm color film by Luc
de Heusch entitled *Magritte ou la leçon des choses*.
The first professional film about Magritte,
it was made for the Ministère de l'Education
Nationale Belge and Radio-Télévision Belge
and released in French, Dutch and English
versions.

1960

In January Magritte was awarded the first
Prix du Couronnement de Carrière. This led
to his being made the subject of a television
programme, "Une visite chez Magritte,"
broadcast by Radio-Télévision Belge
on the evening of February 5.

An exhibition of recent work organized
by Iolas was held at the Galerie Rive Droite
in Paris from February 16 to March 12. Most

of Magritte's output during the year went to Iolas, who was becoming more active in promoting his work.

Suzi Gablik, a young American artist and writer, came to stay with the Magrittes for eight months, to do research for a monograph which was eventually published in 1970.

A retrospective organized by André Bosmans and fellow members of the Verviers group Temps mêlés was held at the Musée des Beaux-Arts, Liège, from October 14 to November 10. It was largely drawn from Belgian collections.

Between December and March 1961 a Magritte retrospective was held in Dallas and Houston. It was organized by Douglas MacAgy, curator at the Dallas Museum for Contemporary Arts (where it was shown from December 8 to January 8), and it was presented in collaboration with the Museum of Fine Arts, Houston (where it was shown from February 2 to March 5).

1961

In one of his least productive years, Magritte painted a mural, about ten oils and ten gouaches; he also resumed making papiers collés.

In May–June the first issue appeared of *Rhétorique*, a review edited by André Bosmans in close collaboration with Magritte, who provided contributions to most of its thirteen issues.

In July–August Magritte painted a mural commissioned by the Government in 1958 for the Salle d'Albertine in the new Palais des Congrès in Brussels.

On September 27 and 28 two rival one-man shows opened in London, one organized by E. L. T. Mesens at the Grosvenor Gallery, the other by James McMullan and Philip M. Laski at the Obelisk Gallery. A number of appreciations by various hands contributed to the Obelisk catalogue, including the most substantial text Breton had yet written about Magritte.

1962

Iolas was active on Magritte's behalf during the year, organizing a show in April–May at his New York gallery and lending works to other exhibitions, although Magritte sold him only a small part of his output.

A large retrospective opened at the Casino Communal in Knokke-le-Zoute on June 30. To coincide with the opening, Marcel Mariën produced and distributed a spoof advertising leaflet ostensibly issued by Magritte which, headed "Grande Baisse," satirized his practice of turning out repeats of his best-selling images.

A retrospective exhibition, "The vision of René Magritte," was held at the Walker Art Center, Minneapolis, from September 16 to October 14.

1963

In July Magritte bought a plot of land in Uccle, the smartest Brussels district, and engaged an architect, Raoul Brunswyck, to draw up plans for a house. After six months of planning by the architect and interference by the client, Magritte abandoned the project, ostensibly on grounds of cost.

1964

The majority of Magritte's oil paintings in 1964 were done for Belgian clients. Iolas, however, remained active in promoting Magritte through exhibitions both in Europe and in America.

A large retrospective was held at the Arkansas Art Center, Little Rock, from May 15 to June 30. Breton wrote the catalogue preface which appeared in French and in an English translation.

1965

Magritte's work in the course of this year was interrupted by illness; his output was somewhat reduced.

A major retrospective, the first to draw fully on both American and European collections, opened at the Museum of Modern Art, New York, in December 1965 and during 1966 was shown at Brandeis, Chicago, Pasadena and Berkeley. Magritte went to New York for the opening of the show and then visited Houston.

In December Patrick Waldberg's monograph, *René Magritte*, was published in Brussels, appearing in French, English and Dutch editions.

E. L. T. Mesens, Paul Delvaux and Magritte in Knokke-le-Zoute, 1962

Opening of the Magritte retrospective at the Casino of Knokke-le-Zoute, June 30, 1962. From left to right: Magritte, Emile Langui and Paul-Gustave van Hecke

Magritte signing a copy of Patrick Waldberg's monograph (Brussels: André de Rache, 1965) for the author

1966

In April the Magrittes spent ten days in Israel at the invitation of the Israeli Ambassador to Belgium, Amiel Najar.

1967

Iolas organized an exhibition of recent work which he had planned to show in all his galleries but which only took place in Paris. It opened on January 10.

Shortly after the Paris show Magritte conceived the idea of making sculpture. By June the eight subjects he had chosen from his own images had been cast in wax by the Bibiesse foundry in Verona and Magritte, who was visiting Italy with Georgette and the Scutenaires, met up with Iolas and traveled to Verona where he made several modifications to the wax casts.

Magritte fell ill shortly after his return from Italy around the end of June. His doctor diagnosed jaundice and in late July or early August, when his condition worsened, he was admitted to the Edith Cavell clinic in Uccle where it was discovered that he was suffering from cancer of the pancreas. The disease was far advanced and the doctors decided not to operate.

A major retrospective was held at the Boijmans Van Beuningen Museum in Rotterdam from August 4 to September 24, after which it went to the Moderna Museet in Stockholm.

Magritte died at home in the early afternoon of August 15. Three days later he was buried in Schaerbeek cemetery.

The Magrittes arriving in New York for the retrospective organized by the Museum of Modern Art, December 1965. From left to right: Harry Torczyner, Georgette and René Magritte, and Peter De Maerel, the Belgian ambassador

Marcel Broodthaers and René Magritte, 1967

This chronology is extracted from the biographical chronology of the catalogue raisonné compiled by David Sylvester, Sarah Whitfield and Michael Raeburn, and is published here by permission of the Menil Foundation.

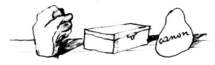
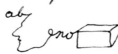

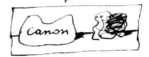

Les Mots et les Images, manuscript. Private collection

Concise Bibliography

Apart from Magritte's own writings and correspondance, this bibliography only contains monographs, articles, catalogues and general works published after the artist's death (1967).

Catalogue Raisonné

SYLVESTER, David, Sarah WHITFIELD and Michael RAEBURN
René Magritte, Catalogue raisonné, 5 vols, Antwerp and Houston: Fonds Mercator, 1992-7.

Writings and Correspondance of Magritte

Texts or letters by Magritte in *Le Fait accompli*, nos. 3, 6, 18, 28, 30, 32, 40, 49, 51-3, 55, 57-8, 67, 76, 78, 81-95, 101, 107, 108-109, 110, 111-113, 120, 127-9, Brussels: Les Lèvres nues, April 1968–March 1975.

Manifestes et autres écrits, Marcel Mariën (ed.), Brussels: Les Lèvres nues, 1972.

Quatre vingt deux lettres de René Magritte à Mirabelle Dors et Maurice Rapin, Paris: Presses du CBE, 1976.

La Destination: lettres à Marcel Mariën (1937-1962), Marcel Mariën (ed.), Brussels: Les Lèvres nues, 1977.

Les Couleurs de la nuit, Marcel Mariën (ed.), Brussels: Les Lèvres nues, 1978.

Ecrits complets, André Blavier (ed.), Paris: Flammarion, 1979.

"Deux écrits inédits," *Cahiers du Musée national d'Art moderne*, no. 1, Paris: Editions du Centre Georges Pompidou, 1979.

Sous le manteau de Magritte (letters to Colinet, James, Mesens, Eluard, etc.), Marcel Mariën (ed.), Fleury-Mérogis: Editions Fantômas, 1984.

Lettres à André Bosmans (1958-1967), Francine Perceval (ed.), Paris: Editions Seghers, 1990.

Magritte / Torczyner: Letters between friends, introduction by Sam Hunter, New York: Harry N. Abrams, 1994.

Works on Magritte

BLAVIER, André
Ceci n'est pas une pipe. Contribution furtive à l'étude d'un tableau de René Magritte, Verviers: Temps mêlés, 1973.

BOUSQUET, Joë
Lettres à Magritte, Le Roeulx: Talus d'approche, 1981.

CALVOCORESSI, Richard
Magritte, Oxford: Phaidon, 1979.

CEULEERS, Jan
René Magritte, 135, rue Esseghem, Jette-Bruxelles, introduction by David Sylvester, Antwerp: Editions Petraco-Pandora, 1999.

DE LULLE, Francis, and Catherine DE CROËS
La Fidélité des images. René Magritte: le cinématographe et la photographie, Brussels: Editions Lebeer-Hossmann, 1976.

DOPAGNE, Jacques
Magritte, Paris: Hazan, 1977.

FOUCAULT, Michel
Ceci n'est pas une pipe, Saint-Clément la Rivière: Fata Morgana, 1973 (first published in *Cahiers du Chemin*, January 1968).

GABLIK, Suzi
Magritte, London: Thames and Hudson, 1970.

GIMFERRER, Pere
Magritte, Barcelona: Poligrafa, 1986.

GOEMANS, Camille
Œuvre 1922-1957, Brussels: André de Rache, 1970.

HAMMACHER, Abraham M.
René Magritte, Paris: Cercle d'art, 1974.

JOUVET, Jean
René Magritte, with an essay by Wieland Schmied, Zurich: Diogenes, 1982.

KONERSMANN, Ralf
René Magritte. Die verbotene Reproduktion, Frankfurt: Fisher Taschenbuch, 1991.

LARKIN, David
Magritte, London: Pan 1972.

LEBEL, Robert
Magritte. Peintures, Paris: Fernand Hazan, 1969.

MARCADÉ, Bernard
René Magritte. Tentative de l'impossible, Brussels: Labor / Isy Brachot, 1992.

MARIËN, Marcel
Apologies de Magritte, Brussels: Didier Devillez, 1994.

MEURIS, Jacques
Magritte, Paris: Casterman, 1989.
René Magritte, Cologne: Benedikt Taschen, 1994.

MICHAUX, Henri
En rêvant à partir de peintures énigmatiques, Saint-Clément la Rivière: Fata Morgana, 1972 (first published in *Mercure de France*, December 1964).

MICHALS, Duane
A Visit with Magritte, Providence: Matrix, 1981.

MÜLLER-TAMM, Pia
René Magritte. Les jours gigantesques, Berlin and Düsseldorf 1996.

NOËL, Bernard
Magritte, Paris: Flammarion, 1976.

NOUGÉ, Paul
René Magritte (in extenso), Brussels: Didier Devillez, 1997.

PAQUET, Marcel
Magritte ou l'éclipse de l'être, Paris: Editions de La Différence, 1982.
Photographies de Magritte, Paris: Contrejour, 1982.
René Magritte, 1898-1967, Cologne: Benedikt Taschen, 1994.

PASSERON, René
René Magritte, Paris: Filipacchi, 1970.

PIERRE, José
Magritte, Paris: Somogy, 1984.

PRATS-OKUYAMA, Catherine
Magritte. Le double secret, Paris: Dessain & Tolra, 1985.

ROBERTS-JONES, Philippe
Magritte poète visible, Brussels: Laconti, 1972.

ROBBE-GRILLET, Alain
La Belle Captive, Brussels: Cosmos, 1975.

ROQUE, Georges
Ceci n'est pas un Magritte. Essai sur Magritte et la publicité, Paris: Flammarion, 1983.

SCHIEBLER, Ralf
Die Kunsttheorie René Magrittes, Munich: Carl Hanser, 1981.

SCHMIED, Wieland
René Magritte: Die Reize der Landschaft, Munich, 1989.

SCHNEEDE, Uwe M.
René Magritte: Leben und Werk, Cologne: DuMont Schauberg, 1973.

SCHREIER, Christoph
René Magritte. Sprachbilder 1927-1930, Hildesheim: Georg Olms, 1985.

SCUTENAIRE, Louis
La Fidélité des images. René Magritte le cinématographe et la photographie, Brussels: Editions Lebeer-Hossmann, 1976.
Avec Magritte, Brussels: Editions Lebeer-Hossmann, 1977.

SOBY, James Thrall
René Magritte, New York: The Museum of Modern Art, 1965.

SYLVESTER, David
Magritte, New York / Washington: Frederick A. Praeger, 1969.
Magritte, New York: Harry N. Abrams, 1992.

TORCZYNER, Harry, and Bella BESSARD
René Magritte: signes et images, Paris: Draeger / Le Soleil noir, 1977.

TORCZYNER, Harry
René Magritte: le véritable art de peindre, Paris: Draeger, 1978.
L'Ami Magritte. Correspondance et souvenirs, Antwerp: Fonds Mercator, 1992.

WALDBERG, Patrick
Magritte. Peintures, Paris: L'Autre Musée, 1983.

WHITFIELD, Sarah
Magritte, London: South Bank Centre, 1992.

Articles on Magritte

BERGER, John
"A Way to Magritte," *New Society*, March 20, 1969, pp. 450-51.

BOUNOURE, V.
"Le thème de la contradiction chez Magritte," *L'Œil*, Paris, February–March 1972, pp. 206-7.

BURY, Pol
"René Magritte ou le viol de la rétine," *Le Quotidien de Paris*, Paris, November 14, 1984, p. 21.

BUTOR, Michel
"Magritte et les mots," *Les Lettres françaises*, Paris, November 13, 1968.

CALAS, E.
"Magritte's Inaccessible Woman," *Artforum*, XVII, New York, March 1979.

CHADWICK, Whitney
"René Magritte and the Liberation of the Image," *Art International*, April 1979, pp. 11-17, 36.

CRUYSMANS, Philippe
"Le visage qui hantait Magritte," *L'Eventail*, Brussels, February 1998, pp. 16-21.

HELD, R. F.
"René Magritte ou le prestidigitateur illusionniste," in *L'Œil du psychanalyste. Surréalisme et surréalité*, Paris: Payot, 1973.

HUBERT, Renée Riese
"The Other Worldly Landscapes of E. A. Poe and René Magritte," *Sub-Stance*, no. 21, 1978, pp. 68-77.
"Henri Michaux et René Magritte," *Stanford French Review*, vol. II, no. 1, 1978, pp. 61-78.

LASCAULT, Gilbert
"Explorations dans la planète Magritte," *Cahiers du Musée national d'Art moderne*, no. 1, Paris, 1979.

LEBEL, Robert
"Avant et après Magritte," *L'Œil*, no. 159, Paris, March 1968.

NOUGÉ, Paul
"Pour illustrer Magritte," *Le Fait accompli*, nos. 34-5, Brussels, April 1970.

SOURIS, André
"Paul Nougé et ses complices," in *Entretiens sur le surréalisme*, Paris / Halle: Mouton, 1968.

VOVELLE, José
"Magritte et le cinéma," *Cahiers de Dada et du surréalisme*, no. 4, Paris: Lettres modernes, 1971, pp. 103-13.

WATSON TAYLOR, Simon
"André Breton and René Magritte," *Studio International*, February 1969, pp. 68-70.

Exhibition Catalogues

René Magritte, Hanover, Kestner-Gesellschaft, 1969; texts by Volker Kahmen, Louis Scutenaire, Wieland Schmied.

Magritte, London, The Tate Gallery, 1969; text by David Sylvester.

Magritte, Tokyo and Kyoto, National Museum of Modern Art, 1971; text by Emile Langui.

La Fidélité des images. René Magritte. Le cinématographe et la photographie, Paris, Musée d'Art moderne de la Ville, 1976; text by Louis Scutenaire.

Magritte, Bordeaux, Capc and Bibliothèque municipale, 1977; texts by Suzi Gablik and Marcel Mariën.

Rétrospective Magritte, Brussels, Palais des Beaux-Arts, 1978 /Paris, Musée National d'Art Moderne, Centre Georges Pompidou, 1979; texts by Jean Clair, Louis Scutenaire, David Sylvester.

Magritte, Paris, Galerie Isy Brachot, 1979; texts by Anne Deknop, Evelyne Kornelis.

René Magritte und der Surrealismus in Belgien, Hamburg, Kunstverein and Kunsthaus, 1982; texts by Marc Dachy, Marcel Mariën, Uwe M. Schneede.

René Magritte, Lausanne, Fondation de l'Hermitage, 1987; texts by Camille Goemans, Marcel Mariën, E.L.T. Mesens *et al.*

René Magritte, Brussels, Musées Royaux des Beaux-Arts, 1988; texts by Louis Scutenaire, André Bosmans, Evelyne Deknop-Kornelis.

René Magritte. Le Domaine enchanté, Basel, Art 88 / Paris, Galerie Isy Brachot, 1988; text by Paul Colinet.

René Magritte 1898-1967, Brussels, Galerie Isy Brachot, 1988; texts by E.L.T. Mesens, Louis Scutenaire, Harry Torczyner *et al.*

René Magritte, Tokyo, National Museum of Modern Art, 1988; texts by Camille Goemans, Marcel Mariën *et al.*

Dessins, croquis et esquisses de l'atelier René Magritte, Paris, Galerie Isy Brachot, 1989; text by Louis Scutenaire.

Magritte 1898-1967, Basel / Paris, Galerie Isy Brachot, 1989; text by Isy Brachot.

Magritte, Madrid, Fundación Juan March, 1989; texts by Camille Goemans, Martine Jaquet, Catherine de Croës, Françoise Daulte, Paul Lebeer.

René Magritte-Photographs, New York, Pace Macgill Gallery, 1990; text by Pierre Sterckx.

René Magritte, Ostend, Provinciaal Museum voor Moderne Kunst, 1990; texts by Marcel Nihoul, Eric Pil, Liliane Sabatini, Willy Van den Bussche.

Magritte, Verona, Galleria Palazzo Fonti, 1991; texts by Giorgio Cortenova, Pierre Sterckx *et al.*

René Magritte: la période Vache, Marseilles, Musée Cantini, 1992; texts by Bernard Blistène, David Sylvester, Sarah Whitfield, Pierre Sterckx *et al.*

Magritte, London, The South Bank Centre, 1992 / New York, The Metropolitan Museum of Art, 1992 / Houston, The Menil Collection, 1992-3 / The Art Institute of Chicago, 1993; monograph by Sarah Whitfield, Ghent: Ludion, 1992.

René Magritte, Peintures et Gouaches, Antwerp, Fondation Ronny Van de Velde, 1994; texts by Jan Ceuleers, David Sylvester, Ronny Van de Velde.

Rétrospective Magritte, Japan, 1994-5; text by Daniel Abadie.

Magritte, Montreal, Museum of Fine Arts, 1996; texts by Alain Cueff, V. Essers, Didier Ottinger, Pierre Sterckx, Harry Torczyner, Bart Verschaffel.

René Magritte, Düsseldorf, Kunstsammlung Nordrhein-Westfalen, 1996; texts by V. Essers, Thomas Heyden, Doris Krystof, K. Lüdeking, Pia Müller-Tamm, Didier Ottinger, Pierre Sterckx.

René Magritte, die Kunst der Konversation, Marcel Broodthaers, Joseph Kosuth, Barbara Bloom …, Düsseldorf, Kunstsammlung Nordrhein-Westfalen, 1996-7, Munich and New York: Prestel, 1996; texts by Barbara Bloom, Marcel Broodthaers, Joseph Kosuth, Didier Ottinger.

René Magritte 1898-1967, Musées Royaux des Beaux-Arts de Belgique, Brussels, 1998; Gisèle Ollinger-Zinque and Frederik Leen (eds.), texts by Alain Berenboom, M. Colin, Jef Cornelis, Carine Fol, Francis de Lulle, Jacques Lust, Paul Raspé, David Sylvester, Harry Torczyner, Anne Wauters, Sarah Whitfield *et al.*

Magritte, Knokke, Casino, 2001; texts by Roger Nellens, Emile Langui, Carine Fol.

Major Exhibitions

Only major group and solo exhibitions organized after Magritte's death (1967) are included in this list.

1968
- "Magritte: cent cinquante œuvres; première vue mondiale de ses sculptures," Galerie Isy Brachot, Brussels, January 19-February 20.
- "Hommage à René Magritte," 41ᵉ Salon du Cercle royal artistique et littéraire de Charleroi, Palais des Beaux-Arts, Charleroi, February 3-25.
- "René Magritte," Byron Gallery, New York, November 19-December 21.

1969
- "Magritte: les 8 sculptures," Galerie Alexandre Iolas, Paris, as of February 7.
- "Magritte," The Tate Gallery, London, February 14-April 2.
- "Ensor, Delvaux, Magritte...," Galerie Gmurzynska, Cologne, March 1-end of April.
- "René Magritte," Kestner Gesellschaft, Hanover, May 8-June 9.
- "René Magritte," Kunsthaus Zurich, June 21-July 27.

1970
- "Cento anni di pittura belga," Galleria Civica d'Arte Moderna, Palazzo dei Diamanti, Ferrara, February 22-April 19.
- "Magritte," Galleria Alberto Schubert, Milan, June 15-July 15.
- "L'Eternel surréalisme (hommage discret à E.L.T. Mesens)," Galerie Isy Brachot, Brussels, October 30-December 7.

1971
- "Retrospective René Magritte," National Museum of Modern Art, Tokyo, May 22-July 11; National Museum of Modern Art, Kyoto, July 20-September 5.
- "Magritte," Galerie Isy Brachot, Knokke-le-Zoute, March 27-April 25.

- "Surréalisme," Bordeaux, Galerie des Beaux-Arts, May 2-September 1.
- "Magritte: sculptures, peintures, gouaches, dessins," Galeries T. Zoumboulakis, Athens, May.
- "The Belgian Contribution to Surrealism," Royal Scottish Academy, Edinburgh, August 21-September 19.

1972
- "Peintres de l'imaginaire: symbolistes et surréalistes belges," Paris, Grand Palais, February 4-April 8.
- "Der Surrealismus 1922-1942," Haus der Kunst, Munich, March 11-May 7; "Le Surréalisme 1922-1942," Musée des Arts décoratifs, Paris, June 9-September 24.
- "Magritte," Banque de Bruxelles, Brussels, May 3-9.

1973
- "Hommage de la ville de Lessines à René Magritte," Hôtel de Ville, Lessines, May 13-27.
- "Magritte," Marlborough Fine Art, London, October 27-November 28.
- "Delvaux, Gnoli, Magritte," Galerie Isy Brachot, Brussels, November 8-December 14.

1974
- "Painters of the Mind's Eye: Belgian Symbolists and Surrealists," The New York Cultural Center, New York, February 1-March 17.
- "Magritte," Davlyn Gallery, New York, November 1974-January 1975.

1976
- "René Magritte: One-Man Show," Art Basel, Galerie Isy Brachot, Basel, June 16-21.
- "Secret Affinities: Words and Images by René Magritte," Institute of the Arts, Rice University, Houston, October 1, 1976-January 2, 1977.

- "La Fidélité des images. René Magritte, le cinématographe et la photographie," Musée d'Art moderne de la Ville, Paris, October-November.

1977
- "René Magritte," Galerie Baukunst, Cologne, April 22-June 25.
- "Magritte," Galerie Levy, Hamburg, spring
- Capc, Bibliothèque municipale, Bordeaux, May 24-July 17.
- "René Magritte: het mysterie van de werkelijkheid," Museum Boijmans Van Beuningen, Rotterdam, August 4-September 24.
- FIAC, Galerie Isy Brachot, Paris, October 21-30.
- "Magritte," Sidney Janis Gallery, New York, December 1-31.
- "René Magritte," Taft Museum, Cincinnati.

1978
- "Dada and Surrealism Reviewed," London, Hayward Gallery, January 11-March 27.
- "Hommage à René Magritte et au surréalisme belge," Salon 1978, Grand Palais, Paris, April 24-May 22.
- "Rétrospective Magritte," Palais des Beaux-Arts, Brussels, October 27-December 31.

1979
- "Magritte 1898-1967," Galerie Isy Brachot, Paris, January 11-March 10.
- "Rétrospective Magritte," Musée National d'Art Moderne, Centre Georges Pompidou, Paris, January 19-April 9.
- "Magritte 1898-1967," Galerie Isy Brachot, Brussels, March 29-May 26.
- "René Magritte: Poetic Images," The Parrish Art Museum, Southampton, N.Y., August 19-September 30.

1981

- "Quatro mestres modernes: De Chirico, Ernst, Magritte, Miró," Museu de Arte, São Paulo, May 18-July 12.
- "Westkunst: zeitgenössische Kunst seit 1939," Messehalle, Cologne, May 29-August 16.

1982

- "René Magritte und der Surrealismus in Belgien," Kunstverein und Kunsthaus, Hamburg, January 23-March 28.
- "René Magritte e il surrealismo in Belgio," Galleria Nazionale d'Arte Moderna, Rome, April 28-July 4.
- "René Magritte et le surréalisme en Belgique," Musées Royaux des Beaux-Arts de Belgique, Brussels, September 24-December 5.
- "René Magritte," Galerie des Arts de Tokyu, Shibuya, Tokyo, August 27-September 15; Prefectural Museum of Art, Toyama, October 9-25; Prefectural Museum of Art, Kumamoto, October 30-December 12.

1983

- "René Magritte," Louisiana Museum, Humlebæk, Denmark, September 15, 1983-January 8, 1984.

1984

- "René Magritte," Kunstsentret, Sonja Henie Foundation, Høvikodden, January 21-March 11.
- "Magritte," Galerie Isy Brachot, Paris, February 22-April 21.
- "Hommage à Magritte," Centre Wallonie-Brussels, Paris, November 1984-February 1985.

1986

- "Le surréalisme en Belgique I," Galerie Isy Brachot, Paris, April 16-July 10.
- "René Magritte," Galleria Civiche d'Arte Moderna, Palazzo dei Diamanti, Ferrara, June 30-October 12.
- "René Magritte: Paintings," Arnold Herstand, New York, November 6-December 20.

1987

- "René Magritte," Fondation de l'Hermitage, Lausanne, June 19-November 1.
- Kunsthalle der Hypo-Kulturstiftung, Munich, November 13, 1987-February 14, 1988.

1988

- "Rétrospective Magritte (1898-1967) dans les collections privées," Galerie Isy Brachot, Brussels, January 20-March 27.
- "René Magritte," Prefectural Museum of Art, Yamaguchi, April 8-May 15; National Museum of Modern Art, Tokyo, May 21-July 10.

1989

- "Magritte 1898-1967," Art Basel, Galerie Isy Brachot, Basel, June 13-19.
- "Magritte 1898-1967," Galerie Isy Brachot, Paris, September 13-December 2.
- Fundación Juan March, Madrid.

1990

- Provinciaal Museum voor Moderne Kunst, Ostend.
- "René Magritte: paintings/drawings/sculptures," Pace Gallery, New York, May 11-June 30.

1991

- "da Magritte a Magritte," Galleria d'Arte Moderna di Palazzo Forti, Verona, July 6-October 20.

1992

- "René Magritte: la période 'vache'," Musée Cantini, Marseilles, February 28-May 3.
- "Magritte," Hayward Gallery, London, May 21-August 2.
- "Magritte," Metropolitan Museum of Art, New York, September 9-November 22.
- "Magritte," Menil Collection, Houston, December 15, 1992-February 21, 1993.

1993

- Galerie Isy Brachot, Brussels.
- "Magritte," Art Institute, Chicago, March 16-May 30.

1994

- Ronny Van de Velde Foundation, Antwerp.
- Retrospective Japan: Mitsukoshi, Hyogo and Fukuoka 1994-5.

1996

- "Le legs Scutenaire, Magritte and Co," Musées Royaux des Beaux-Arts, Brussels.
- Museum of Fine Arts, Montreal, June 20-October 27.
- "Ce qui est attirant est beau," Musées Royaux des Beaux-Arts, Brussels, September 13-December 15.

1997

- "Magritte en Compagnie. Du bon usage de l'irrévérence," Centre culturel de la Communauté française Le Botanique, Brussels.

1998

- Musées Royaux des Beaux-Arts, Brussels, March 6-June 28.
- Galerie Christine et Isy Brachot, Brussels, as of May 3.

1999

- Louisiana Museum of Modern Art, Humlebæk, Denmark, August 6-November 28.

2000

- Museum of Modern Art, San Francisco, May 5-September 5.

2001

- "Magritte," Casino, Knokke-le-Zoute, June 17-September 16.

2002

- "La révolution surréaliste," Musée National d'Art Moderne, Centre Georges Pompidou, Paris, March 6-June 24.
- Bunkamura Museum of Art, Tokyo, July 6-August 25.
- Nagoya City Art Museum, September 1-October 20.
- Hiroshima Museum of Art, October 26-December 8.

2003

- "Magritte," Galerie nationale du Jeu de Paume, Paris, February 10-June 9.

Photographic Credits

Color separations, printing and binding:
Die Keure, Bruges